INTERFAITH DIALOGUE
IN PRACTICE

CHRISTIAN • MUSLIM • JEW

Edited by

Daniel S. Brown, Jr.

Rockhurst University Press
Kansas City, Missouri

ISBN 978-1-886761-32-2

All quotations from the Qur'an are from the translation by
Abdullah Yusuf Ali, published by Tahrike Tarsile Qur'an, Inc.

Manufactured in the United States of America
Printing by Spangler Graphics
Kansas City, Kansas

54321
First Edition

Rockhurst University Press
1100 Rockhurst Road
Kansas City, Missouri 64110
www.rockhurstpress.org

CONTENTS

Acknowledgments

It has been my honor to labor with the women and men whose scholarly work is featured in these pages. Collectively they represent the forefront of reflective thinking about interfaith dialogue within the field of communication studies. This is a book that represents multiple voices. For each of these voices I am thankful. I commend to you their work.

This book began as a series of panel and paper presentations over the course of several annual conferences of the Religious Communication Association. To the conference program planners and the lively participants who contributed to those discussions and to our thinking about interfaith dialogue, I say thank you.

The Director of Rockhurst University Press, Wilburn T. "Bill" Stancil, and the Press' editorial board believed early in the importance of this project. For the shepherding of this project I thank the fine folks at Rockhurst.

I have benefited directly from the encouragement of several colleagues at my home institution, Grove City College. Provost William P. Anderson encouraged me profoundly as I pursued questions related to interfaith dialogue. Likewise, former dean of Grove City College's Calderwood School of Arts and Letters Charles W. Dunn, now at Regent University, shaped my thinking about scholarly publishing. My departmental colleagues Jennifer A. Scott, Kimberly M. Miller, and Lisa Cantini-Seguin provided encouragement, perspective, and scholarly insights to this edited project. My spiritual mentors, who are also the executive leadership team at Sandy Lake Wesleyan Church, provided me an ongoing sense of groundedness and purpose in the context of a genuine religious community.

Without doubt this project would not be as strong as it is without the support of Jared M. Smith, who served well the readers of this volume. His insight and eye-for-detail made him the perfect research and editorial assistant. Jared was a Fellow for the Center for Vision and Values; he also served as the executive administrative editor of the Grove City College *Journal of Law & Public Policy*. Gerald J. "Jack" Hickly III stepped into the role of research assistant late in this project, bringing his organizational expertise to the volume.

Finally, thank you to my family, especially my wife, Susan, and her mother, Delores. Your patience and authenticity make me a better person.

I want to know better what it means to love the Lord my God with all of my heart, soul, mind, and strength (cf. Mark 12:30 and Deuteronomy 6:5).

Daniel S. "Dann" Brown, Jr., Ph.D.
Grove City, Pennsylvania

FUNCTION AND VALUE OF INTERFAITH DIALOGUE

Kathleen M. Edelmayer

For years, interfaith dialogue has been a high priority for religious and secular groups in the United States, Canada, and the world. After the September 11, 2001, terrorist attacks on the United States, and as many Americans became more aware of Islam, the need for understanding of and respect for religious differences has been magnified. Interfaith dialogue has moved to the forefront with an urgency to include Muslims at the table of dialogue.

While most works on interfaith dialogue have addressed the subject from theological, sociological, or political perspectives, *Interfaith Dialogue in Practice: Christian, Muslim, Jew* offers a different way of thinking about interfaith dialogue. The academic field of communication studies has much to offer those who are interested in interfaith dialogue. By employing a communication perspective, this collection of essays examines the use of language, the creation of messages and meaning, and the strategies used by communicants in order to develop their discourse and attempt to influence their audience. Communication is at the heart of interfaith dialogue. While theology may ground messages, and sociological and political factors may affect experience, it is through communication that individuals and groups engage each other and seek meaning and, ideally, respect and understanding.

While interfaith dialogue is certainly not a new concept, it has evolved over the years. In order to understand the significance of interfaith dialogue today, and the context in which our current authors write, it is necessary to examine key historical developments in religious diversity in the United States and in interfaith dialogue. In an effort to provide a backdrop for the essays contained in this book, this foreword examines American religious diversity, developments in interfaith dialogue, and the function and value of interfaith dialogue in America today.

American Religious Diversity

As an immigrant nation, the United States touts diversity as a core value and its religious diversity is well known. The country's respect for religious diversity is embodied in the Constitution's freedom of religion guarantee. It has been a struggle, however, to translate these ideals into concrete behaviors and policies. Although many today describe the United States as a country based on "Judeo-Christian" traditions, this interpretation is relatively recent. In fact, from its founding, the United States was primarily composed of individuals from Protestant Christian traditions.[1] The U.S. experienced an influx of Jewish and Catholic immigrants during the early nineteenth century, but these religious groups were not welcomed; they experienced much discrimination and many difficulties. Only after decades of struggle did the country begin to weave these groups into the fabric of American life; during the 19th century the United States began to shift culturally from "Protestant-Establishment" to "Judeo-Christian."[2]

Historically, immigration policies in the United States were based on quotas; western and northern European nations received the highest priority.[3] For this reason, most immigrants reflected a Judeo-Christian heritage. This changed dramatically in 1965 when President Lyndon Johnson signed the Immigration and Nationality Act. At the October 3, 1965, signing ceremony, President Johnson spoke of the bill's significance: "it does repair a very deep and painful flaw in the fabric of American justice. It corrects a cruel and enduring wrong in the conduct of the American Nation."[4] Until then, "only three countries were allowed to supply 70 percent of all the immigrants" to the United States.[5] After its passage, the United States naturally saw a marked increase in the diversity of immigrants; this in turn fostered ethnic, national, and religious diversity.

The impact of the 1965 bill is still evident today. According to the Pluralism Project at Harvard University, since the 1960s the "new immigrants" have come from Africa, Asia, Latin America, and the Middle East and are Catholic, Muslim, Hindu, and Buddhist.[6] As such, the religious fabric in the United States is changing again. The Pew Forum's 2007 U.S. Religious Landscape Survey found that the number of

Americans who report themselves as members of Protestant denominations is barely 51 percent.[7] Only as a result of immigrants from Central and Latin American nations is Catholicism retaining its proportion at 25 percent of the population.[8] While non-Christian religions currently compose less than 5 percent of the U.S. population, that percentage will continue to grow as a result of immigration.[9] Already, the Pew study notes that two-thirds of U.S. Muslims are immigrants and eight in ten U.S. Hindus are immigrants.[10] In the United States, the need for interfaith dialogue increases as the nation's religious diversity expands.

Historical Developments in Interfaith Dialogue

The 1960s not only saw dramatic changes in immigration policies, it was also a critical time in the development of interfaith dialogue, most evidenced by the Second Vatican Council, or Vatican II. An important focus of Vatican II was its emphasis on ecumenical relationships and the importance of dialogue between the major world religions, particularly between the Catholic Church and Judaism.[11] Pope Paul VI wrote that dialogue "is demanded by the dynamic course of action which is changing the face of modern society. It is demanded by the pluralism of society, and by the maturity man [sic] has reached in this day and age."[12] Interfaith dialogue seeks to bring together those of different religious faiths to develop understanding, to encourage mutual respect, and to work cooperatively in their communities. By pursuing mutual understanding, participants hope that stereotypes, extremism, and intolerance can be minimized and ultimately, perhaps, eliminated. Pope Paul VI recognized respect is inherent in interfaith dialogue: "Moreover, the very fact that he [man] [sic] engages in a dialogue of this sort is proof of his consideration and esteem for others, his understanding and his kindness. He detests bigotry and prejudice, malicious and indiscriminate hostility, and empty, boastful speech."[13]

Ecumenical dialogue has been a high priority for the Vatican since Vatican II, and it was particularly apparent during the papacy of John Paul II who "made more efforts than any other pope in history to improve relations between Roman Catholicism and the Jewish people."[14] Specifically, he "was the first pope to visit the Rome synagogue, which is only a few kilometers from the Vatican. Last September [1993], he was the first pope since the founding of Israel to give an audience to a chief rabbi of the Jewish state. In January [1994], the Vatican and Israel agreed to establish full diplomatic relations with each other."[15] His efforts were not limited to Catholic-Jewish relations; they extended to all faiths. Here, too, he acted "more than any pontiff in modern history."[16] John Paul II "advanced the church's sometimes-difficult relations with Islam by visiting a mosque, speaking to Muslim groups on his foreign trips and insisting on full religious freedom in countries under Islamic law."[17] He called the first World Day of Prayer in 1986. Held in Assisi, Italy, it was truly ecumenical as leaders from many of the world's major religions participated.[18] Throughout his tenure, "Pope John Paul sought to draw representatives of all religions into deeper mutual understanding, respect and dialogue about shared values and beliefs."[19]

International work on interfaith dialogue is not unique to the Vatican. In 1978, Professor Leonard Swidler of Temple University founded the International Scholars Abrahamic Trialogue (ISAT), an international group of scholars representing Jews, Christians, and Muslims. Over 30 years, the ISAT has sponsored conferences throughout the world, established the Global Dialogue Institute, and "translated the cutting-edge research in JES [*Journal of Ecumenical Studies*] into concrete activities and partnerships."[20]

In the United States, the developments in interfaith dialogue have generally paralleled demographic developments in the American religious landscape, though at a much slower rate. Historically, most research on interfaith dialogue has addressed Christian-Jewish relations, with some attention devoted to relations between Christians (Protestant, Orthodox, and Catholic) and/or between specific Christian denominations and Jewish believers. Given the growing number of Muslims in America, it is critical that interfaith dialogue includes Muslims as well, thus embracing "trialogue."

A number of local, national, and international organizations continue to promote interfaith dialogue and acceptance of religious diversity including: The Pluralism Project; the Scarboro Missions (based in Scarborough, Ontario); The Interfaith Alliance (Washington, D.C.); Council for a Parliament of the World's Religions (Chicago); International Interfaith Centre (Oxford, England); North American Interfaith Network; and the Interfaith Youth Core (Chicago). All of these organizations have websites devoted to providing information and promoting dialogue, thus making many resources readily available to individuals and groups interested in developing interfaith dialogue. Web-only resources, such as the Jewish-Christian-Islamic Virtual Media Library, are also available for public use.

The Function and Value of Interfaith Dialogue Today

In the United States, misinformation and destructive stereotypes spread after September 11, 2001, creating prejudice, distrust, and backlash against Muslims. In this post-September 11th society, the Muslim religion has become a basis for animosity, hatred, and division. Fear, misinformation, and ignorance contribute to these reactions, creating a breeding ground for hatred. Such bias is not only experienced by Muslims, however. Hannah Rosenthal, the U.S. State Department's Special Envoy to Monitor and Combat Anti-Semitism, testified in 2011 that "More than six decades after the end of the Second World War, anti-Semitism is still alive and well, and evolving into new, contemporary forms of religious hatred, racism, and political, social and cultural bigotry. According to reports done by the governments of Norway, Germany, Italy, and the United Kingdom there is a disturbing increase in anti-Semitism."[21] Christian believers are also subject to hostility because of their faith. The Pew Forum on Religion and Public Life, for example, reported in 2011 that "More than 2.2 billion people—nearly a third (32 percent) of the world's total population of 6.9 billion—live in countries where either government restrictions on religion or social hostilities involving religion rose substantially over the three-year period studied."[22] Judgmental, callous, and divisive rhetoric and behavior are still targeted at some members of all faiths. As such, the need for interfaith dialogue in the United States and internationally is great.

Fortunately there has been an increased emphasis on interfaith dialogue and unity since 2001. Hajer ben Hadj Salem argues that

September 11, 2011, also became a turning point for Muslims in the United States.[23] He notes that while a number of Muslim organizations designed to create "networks and securing a public space for themselves on the American soil"[24] had been active in the United States, including the Muslim Student Association, the Islamic Society of North America, and the Islamic Circle of North America, the focus of immigrant Muslims was not "to make Islam part of the intellectual heritage of the US."[25] Instead, the goal of self-appointed leaders was "to revive Islamic civilization throughout the world, including the United States."[26] These organizations focused their efforts inward to the Muslim community, not outward to non-Muslims. After 9/11, Salem continues, Muslims engaged in interfaith dialogue to teach "their religious beliefs and seek their [non-Muslim neighbors'] support and protection. The interfaith open house became as regular an affair as religious observances."[27]

A challenge facing each wave of immigration is how to weave together tradition, culture, and faith with American culture. Each group experiences unique challenges. In earlier years, with an emphasis on the "melting pot," newcomers were expected to integrate their faith seamlessly into established American customs. Later, U.S. diversity was described metaphorically as a "tossed salad"; immigrants should be able to retain and celebrate their own identities. An unintentional consequence of the tossed salad metaphor resulted from its emphasis on difference, leading many authors to suggest a new metaphor: "tapestry." The American tapestry is developed from the various peoples, ethnicities, and religions weaving their unique characteristics into an integrated, interdependent, diverse fabric that celebrates the values of diversity as expressed in the U.S. Constitution. Interfaith dialogue is one way to learn about religious differences in order to uphold, value, and respect each other.

<><><><><><><><><><><><><><><><><><><><><>

Unique Focus of This Text

At the start of the twenty-first century, technology, travel, government policies, multi-national corporations, and immigration continue to break down barriers and distance between countries and ethnicities. No longer is our "neighbor" next door to us; now our "neighbor" can be halfway around the world (or our next door neighbor may have emigrated from halfway around the world!). The need for inter-faith dialogue continues to grow as we interact with people of different faiths. Worldwide, Muslims are the second largest religious group, and yet, in many areas of the world, they are misunderstood. Dialogue can no longer be limited to Christian denominations and the Jewish traditions. Dialogue must include all major religions and must be at all levels: interpersonal, organizational, public, and mediated.

This particular volume addresses a gap in the current literature on interfaith dialogue in its focus, theoretical perspective, and level of dialogue. First, the volume's central focus is dialogue within the three Abrahamic religions (Judaism, Christianity, and Muslim). Second, every essay examines interfaith dialogue from a communication perspective. Communication scholars Kimberly A. Pearce and W. Barnett Pearce note that public dialogue should be "collaborative problem solving, appreciation for different perspectives, and identification of common ground."[28] Pearce and Pearce's assumptions are implicitly, sometimes explicitly, apparent in the chapters contained herein as the authors examine the elements of language, listening strategies, and the impact of personal experience on interaction. Third, the works contained in this volume focus on interfaith dialogue at the local and interpersonal levels. We understand groups different from ourselves through our individual encounters—whether the differences are based on race, ethnicity, gender, or religion. That is, our individual, interpersonal experiences affect our understanding about people, events, and institutions more so than our understanding from an abstract, theoretical level.

The goal of dialogue is not consensus, but rather understanding.[29] Genuine dialogue "is to hear and to better understand each others' pain and what it is that hurts each other, for there are the wounds of past injustices and, precisely there, the wounds from which new life can emerge."[30] This, indeed, is the purpose of interfaith dialogue at all levels—to increase understanding, to heal wounds, and to bring together "them" and "us" to become "we." May this volume likewise contribute to that noble purpose.

◇◇◇◇◇◇◇◇◇◇◇◇◇◇◇◇◇◇◇◇◇◇◇◇◇◇◇◇◇◇◇◇◇

Notes

[1]Hajer ben Hadj Salem, "A Golden Opportunity: Religious Pluralism and American Muslim Strategies of Integration in the US after 9/11, 2001," *Journal for the Study of Religions and Ideologies* 9, no. 27 (2010): 246-60.

[2]Ibid.

[3]U.S. Department of State Office of the Historian, "The Immigration Act of 1924 (The Johnson-Reed Act)." http://history.state.gov/milestones/1921-1936/ ImmigrationAct.

[4]Lyndon B. Johnson, "Remarks at the Signing of the Immigration Bill," Lyndon Baines Johnson Library and Museum. Liberty Island, N.Y., October 3, 1965. http:// www.lbjlib.utexas.edu/johnson/archives.hom/speeches hom/651003.asp.

[5]Ibid.

[6]The Pluralism Project at Harvard University (www.pluralism.org).

[7]The Pew Forum on Religion and Public Life, "U.S. Religious Landscape Survey, 2007," http://religions.pewforum.org/reports (accessed March 3, 2012). A PDF version of the full report can also be accessed at: http://religions. pewforum.org/pdf/report-religious-landscape-study-full.pdf.

[8]Ibid.

[9]Ibid.

[10]Ibid.

[11]See Elizabeth T. Groppe, "Revisiting Vatican II's Theology of *The People of God* After Forty-five Years of Catholic-Jewish Dialogue," *Theological Studies* 72 (2011): 586-619; John W. O'Malley, *What Happened at Vatican II* (Cambridge, MA: Belknap Press, 2008).

[12]Pope Paul VI. *Ecclesiam Suam*. Last modified August 6, 1964. http:// www.vatican.va/holy_father/paul_vi/encyclicals/documents/hf_p-vi_ enc_06081964_ecclesiam_en.html, para 78.

[13]Ibid., para 79.

[14]"Vatican Courage," *Baltimore Jewish Times*, April 8, 1994.

[15]Ibid.

[16]Jerry Filteau, "Pope Made Important Overtures to non-Christian Religions," *Catholic News Service*, 2005. http://www.catholicnews.com/jpii/ stories/story04.htm. This article provides an extensive list of Pope John Paul II's efforts, with particular attention to Catholic-Muslim relations.

[17]Ibid.

[18]Ibid. Also see John Paul II, "Address of John Paul II to the Representatives of the Christian Churches and Ecclesial Communities Gathered in Assisi for the

World Day of Prayer." October 27, 1986. http://www.vatican.va/holy_father/ john_paul_ii/speeches/1986/october/documents/hf_jp-ii_spe_19861027_ prayer-peace-assisi_en.html.

[19]Ibid.

[20]See http://institute.jesdialogue.org/about/history/.

[21]Hannah Rosenthal, "Combating Anti-Semitism in the OSCE Region: Taking Stock of the Situation Today," Statement before the Commission on Security and Cooperation in Europe (U.S. Helsinki Commission), Washington, D.C., December 2, 2011. http://www.state.gov/j/drl/rls/rm/2011/178164.htm.

[22]Pew Forum on Religion and Public Life, "Rising Restrictions on Religion," August 9, 2011. http://www.pewforum.org/Government/Rising-Restrictions-on-Religion(2).aspx.

[23]Salem, "A Golden Opportunity."

[24]Ibid., 253.

[25]Ibid., 252.

[26]Ibid., 252-53.

[27]Ibid., 254.

[28]W. Barnett Pearce and Kimberly A. Pearce, "Taking a Communication Perspective on Dialogue," in *Dialogue: Theorizing Difference in Communication Studies,* eds. Rob Anderson, Leslie A. Baxter, and Kenneth N. Cissna (Thousand Oaks, CA: Sage, 2003), 39-56. http://www.pearceassociates.com/essays/comm_ perspective.htm.

[29]Anne Hunt, "Interfaith Dialogue: Lessons from the Ecumenical Movement," *Compass* (2009, November 12): 8-13.

[30]Ibid.

◇◇◇◇◇◇◇◇◇◇◇◇◇◇◇◇◇◇◇◇◇◇◇◇◇◇◇◇◇◇◇

Bibliography

Adams, Carey, Charlene Berquist, Randy Dillon, and Gloria Galanes. "CMM and Public Dialogue: Practical Theory in a Community-wide Communication Project." *Human Systems: The Journal of Systemic Consultation and Management* 15 (2004): 115-26. http://pearceassociates.com/essays/documents documents/84954_MissouriUni.pdf.

Dillon, Michele. "2009 Association for the Sociology of Religion Presidential Address: Can Post-secular Society Tolerate Religious Differences?" *Sociology of Religion* 71 (2010): 139-56.

Eck, Diana. "From Diversity to Pluralism." In *On Common Ground: World Religions in America.* New York: Columbia University Press, 2006. http://pluralism.

org/pluralism/essays/from_diversity_to_pluralism.php.

Filteau, Jerry. "Pope Made Important Overtures to non-Christian Religions." *Catholic News Service,* 2005. http://www.catholicnews.com/jpii/stories/story04.htm.

Groppe, Elizabeth T. "Revisiting Vatican II's Theology of The People of God After Forty-five Years of Catholic-Jewish Dialogue." *Theological Studies* 72 (2011): 586- 619.

Haney, Marsha Snulligan. "Envisioning Islam: Imam Mohammed and Interfaith Dialogue." *The Muslim World* 99 (2009): 608-34.

Hunt, Anne. "Interfaith Dialogue: Lessons from the Ecumenical Movement." *Compass* (November 12, 2009): 8-13.

Johnson, Lyndon B. "Remarks at the Signing of the Immigration Bill." Lyndon Baines Johnson Library and Museum. Liberty Island, N.Y., October 3, 1965. http://www.lbjlib.utexas.edu/johnson/archives.hom/speeches.hom/651003.asp.

Mojzes, Paul, and Leonard Swidler. "Common Elements of Judaism, Christianity, and Islam." *Journal of Ecumenical Studies* 39 (2002): 80-81.

O'Malley, John W. *What Happened at Vatican II.* Cambridge, MA: Belknap Press, 2008.

Paul VI, Pope. *Ecclesiam Suam.* Last modified August 6, 1964. http://www.vatican.va/holy_father/paul_vi/encyclicals/documents/hf_p-vi_enc_06081964_ecclesiam_en.html.

Pearce, W. Barnett, and Kimberly A. Pearce. "Taking a Communication Perspective on Dialogue." *In Dialogue: Theorizing Difference in Communication Studies,* edited by Rob Anderson, Leslie A. Baxter, and Kenneth N. Cissna, 39-56. Thousand Oaks, CA: Sage, 2003. http://www.pearceassociates.com/essays/comm_perspective.htm.

The Pew Forum on Religion and Public Life, "U.S. Religious Landscape Survey, 2007," http://religions.pewforum.org/reports.

————. "Rising Restrictions on Religion." August 9, 2011. http://www.pewforum.org/Government/Rising-Restrictions-on-Religion(2).aspx.

Rosenthal, Hannah. "Combating Anti-Semitism in the OSCE Region: Taking Stock of the Situation Today." Statement before the Commission on Security and Cooperation in Europe (U.S. Helsinki Commission). Washington, D.C., December 2, 2011. http://www.state.gov/j/drl/rls/rm/2011/178164.htm.

Salem, Hajer ben Hadj. "A Golden Opportunity: Religious Pluralism and American Muslim Strategies of Integration in the US after 9/11, 2001." *Journal for the Study of Religions and Ideologies* 9 (2010): 246-60.

Swidler, Leonard. "Trialogue: Out of the Shadows into Blazing 'Desert' Sun."

Journal of Ecumenical Studies 45 (2010): 493-509.

———. "Can Interreligious Dialogue Make a Difference?" *Journal of Ecumenical Studies* 43, no. 2 (2008): 1-4.

———. "Islam and the Trialogue of Abrahamic Traditions." *Cross Currents* 42 (1992-93): 444-452.

U.S. Department of State Office of the Historian. "The Immigration Act of 1924 (The Johnson-Reed Act)." http://history.state.gov/milestones/1921-1936/ImmigrationAct.

Chapter One

FAMILY MATTERS FOR THE CHILDREN OF ABRAHAM

Daniel S. Brown, Jr.

One God: The transcendent Creator who is eternal, omnipotent, omniscient, and omnipresent.
One man: Abraham
One promise: "I will establish my covenant as an everlasting covenant between me and you and your descendants after you for the generations to come, to be your God and the God of your descendants after you." *(Genesis 17:7)*
Two sons: Isaac and Ishmael
Three religions: Judaism, Christianity, and Islam

◇◇◇◇◇◇◇◇◇◇◇◇◇◇◇◇◇◇◇◇◇◇◇◇◇◇◇◇◇◇◇◇

Interfaith Dialogue is Communication

From the first polite greetings to the tension-filled conversations, from the light laughter to the goodbye hugs, from the new friendships to the lingering doubts, interfaith dialogue takes place in the world of symbols. Interfaith dialogue happens among humans who are bound to each other by linguistic bartering systems. It *is* communication. Interestingly, this volume is the first attempt by communication and media scholars to explore what works, and doesn't work, in interfaith dialogue from a communication perspective.

We know, frankly, what doesn't work. Listening to experts pontificate as talking heads, engaging in listserve discussion groups, and prowling for absurd ambitions like "achieving world peace by the end of next week" do not work. In the pages that follow we are introduced to a series of essays that provide examples of what works in interfaith dialogue. Much more could be written, and it will be. This is only the first book produced by communication and media scholars writing from their disciplinary perspectives about the dialogue that takes place, or should take place, between the Abrahamic faiths.

In this opening essay, I propose to set the stage for the chapters that follow by exploring two questions the reader surely has in mind: What are the Abrahamic faiths? What is interfaith dialogue?

Characterizing the Abrahamic Faiths

The Abrahamic faiths—Judaism, Christianity, and Islam—representing the three monotheistic world religions, are intertwined with a shared history, many common values, and unique theological assumptions that distinguish them from non-Abrahamic religious faiths.

The three faith families agree on much:
1. There is only One God who is the Creator and Ruler of the universe.
2. There is an afterlife.
3. God is absolute reality and truth.
4. God reveals himself through his prophets and through their writings.
5. God will ultimately intervene in history and bring judgment to all people and nations.
6. Humans are responsible moral agents who choose between right and wrong.
7. Humans are created in the image of God.
8. Human life is sacred.

The Abrahamic faiths nevertheless also share a troubled past and present, marked by mistrust, hatred, and even war. The media world is replete with examples of faith-motivated hatred and violence. Wars and rumors of wars. Terrorism and accusations of terrorism. Boycotts and threats of boycotts. How sad that the wars, acts of terror, even the seemingly benign boycotts are conducted in the name of God. How grievous that Jews, Christians, and Muslims turn against each other in the name of their God. They are, after all, part of the family; they are children of Abraham.

More than half of the world's population is part of the Abrahamic faith tradition. Roughly speaking, a bit less than 55 percent of humanity worships within the framework of the three Abrahamic faiths. Thirty percent of the world's population are members of other, typically non-monotheistic, religious faiths, and just less than 15 percent do not claim a religious belief system or affiliation. Christianity is today the largest religion in the world. Islam is the world's second largest religion. The Jewish tradition is the oldest of the monotheistic faiths, and both Christianity and Islam borrow heavily from Jewish thought and theory.[1] Together, they are referred to as the Abrahamic faiths because each traces the beginning of its religion to one man: Abraham. The Abrahamic relationship differs by nature in each case, however.

The connection with Abraham is sometimes physical, sometimes spiritual, or sometimes both physical and spiritual. People of the Jewish faith have a physical relationship or connection with their father Abraham. Jewish believers trace their lineage through Isaac, Abraham's second son, whose mother was Sarah. Moses the Lawgiver was descended from Abraham through Isaac, born six generations after Abraham. It was Moses who led the children of Israel out of their Egyptian captivity when he had reached maturity. Torah teaches the Jews that they are part of God's everlasting covenant. They are the literal, physical children or seed of Abraham.

People of the Christian faith understand that theirs is a spiritual relationship with Abraham. Christianity was born as a sect of Judaism. While most first century Christian believers were Jewish, the religion quickly expanded to include the Gentiles of the world. The Apostle Paul teaches in his letter to the Galatian believers that through faith in Jesus the Christ they "clothed" themselves with Christ. There is no longer "Jew nor Gentile, neither slave nor free, nor is there male and female." No, wrote Paul, if you belong to Christ, "then you are Abraham's seed, and heirs according to the promise" (Galatians 3:26-29). The Christian scriptures teach that Christians are Abraham's seed and participate in the everlasting covenant that God himself promised. God's promise to Abraham, according to the Christian scriptures, is to his spiritual seed, not his physical seed. Christians are the children of Abraham in a real, yet spiritual, sense.

People of the Islamic faith have both a physical and a spiritual relationship to their father Abraham. The people who would first hear Muhammad's message in the Arabian peninsula were, in fact, descended from Abraham's first son, Ishmael, born of Hagar. Christians and Muslims believe that Jesus was a descendant of Abraham through Isaac, while Muslims also recognize that Muhammad was a descendant through Ishmael. In addition to the physical, genetic lineage to Abraham-as-father, Muslims hold Abraham in high regard as a prophet. Abraham was the first monotheistic believer; he was the first to make a pilgrimage to Mecca. Because Abraham was the first to worship and follow the One True God, he is the spiritual father of all who do likewise. All who honor Abraham's true teaching and understand that there is only One God are spiritually allied to him; Muslims are of his spiritual and physical descendants or seed.

All things considered, the children born into the Abrahamic family do not historically "play well together." The phenomenon is not unlike other forms of sibling rivalry, if we are to be honest. With a fair amount of consistency humans demonstrate a natural tendency toward collective guilt and collective revenge. When a person or group suffers a hurt or a perceived wrong, there is an inclination to avenge the wound. Frequently, the individual or the specific group that created the hurt or the wrong is unavailable, and vengeance is meted out to the family or category of people with which the original agent is presumably identified. So, the wound of an enemy frequently results in vengeance on the enemy's nation, tribe, clan, family, or religious community. It is not right, but it happens in families every day. Sadly, it makes sense in a distorted way because it seems often to benefit the avenger with minimal loss of life, dignity, or power. We do not regularly hold our brothers and sisters to account when they lash out against a group because of a single person's actions. Perhaps the rules by which we play need to change.

Understanding Interfaith Dialogue

Popular and scholarly interest in interfaith dialogue is complex and increasingly ubiquitous. The controlling vision of this volume is that interfaith dialogue is best imagined as an organic process. While there are councils, committees, conferences, and commissions designed to foster or promote interfaith dialogue, the contributors to the current book believe that interfaith dialogue does not require theological heavyweights gathered for academic banter. In fact, we might argue—and some of us do this specifically in our individual contributions to the book—interfaith dialogue is at its best, is most fruitful, and is most effective when non-expert lay people engage with one another. It may be uncomfortable at times, but the task is part of being a person of faith. Our God expects us to be hospitable to others.

The current volume is shaped by the authors' commitment to the research protocols of communication studies. Where other interfaith texts propose to provide theological, political, or sociological insights, all authors in this work are communication scholars who are involved in interfaith dialogue.

As scholars of communication theory, many of us follow in the phenomenological tradition of Russian philosopher Mikhail Bakhtin. Michael Eskin reminds us, "Bakhtin conceives dialogue as an encounter, as the 'dialogic encounter of two consciousnesses.'"[2] Communication is essential if there is to be awareness, understanding, and any sense of belongingness that accompanies the human experience. All humans seek to live consciously. Our striving for personal or communal understanding succeeds only in the context of communication with the other. Bakhtin's term for this human desire is "consciousness." Eskin explains: "Consciousness, Bakhtin stresses, 'consists precisely in [my] encounter with the other. This is the *highest level of sociality*'" (italics in original). Bakhtin suggests that people "'travel' back and forth between each other, performing co-existence as dialogue."[3]

We are in the end doing what humans who are created in God's image must do. We are "performing co-existence as dialogue." Our vision of interfaith dialogue takes place at the breakfast table, among congregants of divergent worship centers, in the classroom, and throughout the community. It may help some readers to think of the practices described in this volume as being interfaith exchanges or interfaith encounters rather than as interfaith dialogue. Bakhtin's explication allows for this. But, let us be clear: the practices described in these pages are dialogue. Everything we say to the religious other is dialogic. Our words, our phrases, our experiences, and our beliefs are shaped in concert with the other. As the world continues to become smaller, by "performing co-existence" we actively interact with the other, that is with those who we are not, in dialogue.

In regard to our individual faiths, dialogue of this type presents a clear challenge that must be faced head-on. We clearly and specifically contend that interfaith dialogue does not exist to create some sort of amalgam, a new or improved religious system. There are those who seek to create religious syncretism. Interfaith dialogue partners are not among these. Syncretism refers to the fusing or melding of divergent, sometimes opposing, beliefs into a new system of belief. As members of distinct faith traditions, we can celebrate our common legacy without the expectation that a new or common core of doctrine will emerge. Judaism, Christianity, and Islam are indeed exclusivist by their very natures. Interfaith dialogue does not seek to change that. Partners in interfaith dialogue accept that while the three faiths have much in common, they are mutually exclusive. Nonetheless, we share a planet and a heritage that we hope to pass on to our children's children and to their grandchildren.

The late Anglican philosopher-vicar John Stott, the principal framer of the Lausanne Covenant produced in 1974 at the first International Congress on World Evangelization, spoke purposefully and gracefully about the exclusivity of Christianity. The three Abrahamic faiths each comprise exclusivist claims making them, at some level, mutually exclusive ontologically. Stott's observations, given in the context of Christian faith and practice, I believe, are applicable to the vision of interfaith dialogue cast by this volume's contributors. While "tolerance is one of today's most coveted virtues," according to Stott, religionists need to recognize that there are many different kinds of tolerance.[4]

Stott discusses three types of tolerance in his 2003 interview with Gary Barnes.[5] *Legal* tolerance is the first kind. It involves fighting for the equal rights before the law of all ethnic and religious minorities. "Christians," Stott said, "should be at the forefront of this campaign." The second type of tolerance is *social* tolerance. This concept encapsulates "going out of our way to make friends with adherents of other faiths." As human beings who understand that we are created in the image of God, *social* tolerance has much appeal to members of the Abrahamic faiths. This is where most of this volume's authors imagine or re-imagine dialogue taking place. The third kind of tolerance is *intellectual* tolerance. Stott said, "This is to cultivate a mind so broad and open as to accommodate all views and reject none."[6] At the least, *intellectual* pluralism diminishes the truth commitments of the adherents. At its worst, *intellectual* pluralism disembowels all faith traditions leaving them powerless and purposeless.

It is perhaps wise to state specifically what interfaith dialogue does not portend to do. Interfaith dialogue does not seek to resolve or dilute theological issues; it seeks to comprehend. Interfaith dialogue does not seek to convert or proselytize nonbelievers; it seeks to explore and investigate. Interfaith dialogue does not seek to win a debate; it seeks to build respectful understanding in relationship with others.

Armed with these pithy definitions-by-negation, let us now consider what interfaith dialogue does. That is, what can we expect of interfaith dialogue? Let me outline three outcomes of interfaith dialogue that help explain, at least in part, why students of communication and media should study and pursue the practices described in this volume.

First, cooperation begins with understanding the other. We live in an increasingly secular world, one in which religion is hushed in the public square. Religion, we are frequently told, is a private affair with no standing in civil discourse. One of the legitimate criticisms faced in the public square by persons of faith is that we do not get along with each other. If we do not get along with each other, why should any of our voices be welcomed into the public square? Who will listen to the testimony of the faithful if the faithful are dismissive or aggressively intolerant of people of a different faith? Defending and protecting the religious voices of others opens the door to our own voice gaining resonance in public life.

Second, friendship emerges from mutual understanding. Our paths do not frequently cross with the religious others' paths. We often maintain separate social, educational, and service institutions related to our faith traditions. When we drop our façades and join together for a common meal, a joint service project, an integrated learning experience, or just dessert, we might find out that we like each other. This aligns with Stott's conceptualization of *social* tolerance. Abraham is understood by all to have had a special relationship with God. He is described in our holy scriptures as being a "friend of God" (cf. Isaiah 41:8, James 2:27, and An-Nisaa 4:125). Why should we not invest time with one another to form friendships with others who like Abraham seek to be friends of God? Respect for our differences, acceptance of our diversity, elevation of our Creator-God: lifelong friendships are sometimes made of less.

Finally, obedience to God requires us to exercise love and to be hospitable in our interfaith activity. The concept of hospitality emerges early in the Torah when Abraham and his wife Sarah welcome and entertain strangers in his household (Genesis 18). The strangers turn out to be angels and the Lord himself. The Qur'an contains a parallel story involving Abraham and Sarah welcoming angelic strangers (Az-Zariyat 51).

The Jewish law has this clear command: "When a foreigner resides among you in your land, do not mistreat them. The foreigner residing among you must be treated as your native-born. Love them as yourself, for you were foreigners in Egypt. I am the Lord your God (Leviticus 19:33-34). The Qur'an requires believers "to do good—to parents, kinsfolk, orphans, those in need, neighbours who are near, neighbours who are strangers, the companion by your side, the wayfarer… for God loveth not the arrogant, the vainglorious—(Nor) those who are niggardly or enjoin niggardliness on others, or hide the bounties which God hath bestowed on them" (An-Nisaa 4:36-37). The Christian scriptures echo these narratives and proclamations with their own command: "Do not forget to show hospitality to strangers, for by so doing some people have shown hospitality to angels without knowing it" (Hebrews 13:2). Jesus, of course, is known to have summarized the Hebrews' law into two clear commands, both of which resonate with these scriptural themes: "'Love the Lord your God with all your heart and with all your soul and with all your mind.' This is the first and greatest commandment. And the second is like it: 'Love your neighbor as yourself.' All the

Law and the Prophets hang on these two commandments" (Matthew 22:37-40).

For Jews, Christians, and Muslims, what could be more hospitable, more welcoming, than engaging the other in conversation, breaking bread together, and welcoming him or her into our circle of concern with grace and peace? Surely at a minimum, "loving your neighbor as yourself" requires dialogue, that is, "performing co-existence" with the religious other. In practical and spiritual ways people of the Abrahamic faith glorify God and increase their own joy when they exercise hospitality to others, especially those who are geographic or theological neighbors.

We support interfaith dialogue because it leads to cooperation in the community, friendship through associations, and obedience to spiritual commands. As we encounter one another, we engage in the *"highest level of sociality"* to use Bakhtin's phrase. It is by means of language that we "travel" symbolically "between each other" and "co-existence as dialogue." Perhaps we can ultimately know ourselves and our own religious beliefs only in dialogue with the other.

◇◇◇◇◇◇◇◇◇◇◇◇◇◇◇◇◇◇◇◇◇◇◇◇◇◇

Notes

[1]Many trustworthy online resources provide accurate and current demographic information about world religions. Among these is the U.S. Religion Landscape Survey, which is sponsored by the Pew Forum on Religion and Public Life and is available at http://religions.pewforum.org/reports.

[2]Michael Eskin, *Ethics and Dialogue: In the Works of Levinas, Bakhtin, Mandel'shtam, and Celan* (New York: Oxford University Press, 2000), 90.

[3]Ibid.

[4]Gary Barnes, "Why Don't They Listen?" *Christianity Today* 47.9 (2003): 51. I am thankful for Annalee Ward pointing me in the direction of Barnes' interview with Stott in her article, Annalee R. Ward, "Problems and Promise in Pluralism," *Journal of Communication and Religion* 27 (March 2004): 1-10.

[5]Gary Barnes, "Why Don't They Listen?" 51.

[6]Ibid.

◇◇◇◇◇◇◇◇◇◇◇◇◇◇◇◇◇◇◇◇◇◇◇◇◇◇◇◇◇◇

Bibliography

Barnes, Gary. "Why Don't They Listen?" *Christianity Today* 47.9 (2003): 50-52.

Eskin, Michael. *Ethics and Dialogue: In the Works of Levinas, Bakhtin, Mandel'shtam, and Celan.* New York: Oxford University Press, 2000.

Ward, Annalee R. "Problems and Promise in Pluralism." *Journal of Communication and Religion* 27 (March 2004), 1-10.

Chapter 2

ENACTING GRACE AND TRUTH: A COMMUNICATION PERSPECTIVE ON INTERFAITH DIALOGUE BETWEEN THE ABRAHAMIC TRADITIONS

Gerald Driskill and John Gribas

This chapter exists because of W. Barnett Pearce. His commitment to the CMM project in order to create better social worlds has left a lasting legacy. His work in collaboration with Kim Barnett and colleagues (http://www.cmminstitute.net/) continues to shape our world. We write out of a debt of gratitude as we seek to capture key ideas found not only in his writings but also in the way he embodied dialogic ideals. Thank you, Barnett.

The increasing inevitability of interfaith contact is clear, as is the case for more effective interfaith dialogue. In fact, dialogue itself is promoted as the world's hope for peaceful reconciliation in the face of all kinds of entrenched conflicts, including conflicts arising from faith differences. The crucial role of dialogue in promoting human charity has been emphasized through powerful metaphor:

> Dialogue is to love, what blood is to the body. When the flow of blood stops, the body dies. When dialogue stops, love dies and resentment and hate are born. But dialogue can restore a dead relationship. Indeed, this is the miracle of dialogue: it can bring relationship into being, and it can bring into being once again a relationship that has died.[1]

Dialogue, thus, is a prized value and seen as central to life, at least life lived with some degree of collective harmony. Consistent with that value, the chapters composing the content of this book focus on dialogue as a means for improved understanding between the major Abrahamic faith traditions. In this way, specifically, dialogue holds great potential for our world.

We enthusiastically embrace this potential. At the same time we, like so many others, have had experiences that underscore the problematic nature of dialogue. These experiences often involve interfaith sessions characterized by calls for peace and tolerance such as the following paraphrase designed to reflect many actual sentiments we have heard.

> *I want to agree with Rabbi Markus. As he said and my brother, the Rev. Mike, stated, our books say essentially the same thing—we all agree on the need for peace and tolerance.*

We certainly agree on the need to strive for peace and tolerance, but we share a concern that such comments appear to be based on the presumption that most if not all faith-grounded claims are essentially professing "the same thing." Discourse of this kind can inadvertently create monologues, rather than authentic dialogues. It creates monologues because, in the attempt to promote peace, substantive and potentially conflicting aspects of differing faith positions are ignored—perhaps even silenced—through a kind of strategic reframing that morphs positions into a monological similarity (i.e., saying "essentially the same thing"). Rabbi Yoffie summarizes his thirty years of experiences with such interfaith engagement:

> Most of the time—and it is painful for me to admit this—it is terribly boring. Most of the time there is a tendency to manufacture consensus, whether it exists or not. Most of the time we go to great lengths to avoid conflict. . . . And most of the time we are satisfied with mouthing a few noble, often-repeated sentiments. Thus, we affirm the importance of mutual understanding, tolerance and dialogue; we assert that all human beings are created in the image of God; we proclaim that despite our differences, all of our traditions preach love of humankind and service to humanity.[2]

Yoffie goes on to discuss his reasons for staying with the dialogic process and acknowledging what happens at rare moments that make it worth the effort. We will return to his ideas later in this chapter as they resonate with our main thrust. Like Rabbi Yoffie, we seek for ways to move past the pretense of dialogue or, as Buber called it, monologue disguised as dialogue.[3] Such a shift means a move not only from boredom, but also from a kind of oppression noted by Barnett Pearce that may occur in these settings.[4] The shift to true dialogue requires attentiveness to some inherent dialectical tensions that offer challenge in terms of both ethical stance and strategic meaning management.

Concerning ethical stance, we hold that a prescriptive approach to true interfaith dialogue must be grounded in an ethical imperative calling participants to attend to both poles of a tension, such as commonality-difference or certainty-uncertainty. This position is well grounded in various dialectic and dialogic approaches that assert the ethicality of such moves.[5] In particular, Murray synthesizes the role of ethics in both Bakhtin's and Levinas' writings on dialogue and dialectics, stressing the importance of how we respond to the "Other" in an ethical way.

> The dialogue that we are is a dialogue between self and Other, between answerability and the call to responsibility. Moreover, the synthesis of Bakhtinian answerability and Levinasian responsibility reveals the dialogical nature of the phenomenon of ethics. Ethics is itself constituted as a dialogue of voices, of the voices of the Others to whom we are responsible, and of the voice of oneself to whom we are answerable.[6]

Thus, dialogue, to avoid pretense, inherently involves more than just talk or the free exchange of ideas. Dialogue must rely on forms of communication that encourage participants to attend to inherent tensions. For instance, in one study on church cooperation Driskill, Meyer, and Mirivel found that attending to rather than sidestepping both poles of a dialectic tension was viewed by leaders as an ethical stance.[7] In short, they saw the silenced pole of the cooperation-noncooperation as unethical and against the "unity" metanarrative found in the teachings of Jesus. Similarly, Gribas assigned students to religiously diverse groups and tasked them with finding a way to encourage more open, honest, respectful, and peace-promoting communication among members of the campus community with differing belief systems.[8] Through reflection papers, he discovered that many students were disappointed at how little group members were willing to really engage and share faith commitments (or non-commitments). According to the unpublished excerpt of one student participant, as a group we were also a microcosm of the question, and seen in that light, were not nearly as effective at modeling the behaviors we promoted in task discussion. It was not that we were disrespectful as such, but everyone was so careful not to antagonize that, in truth, our own communication was not as open, and therefore honest, as I would have wished.

This student and others seemed to recognize that dealing with the inherent tensions is a necessity for "honest" and thus ethical interfaith dialogue.

At the same time, strategic attentiveness to managing intertwined contexts of meaning is also central to moving away from fake toward genuine dialogue. In other words, individuals need to act with an awareness of multiple interpretive contexts in a way that frees them to understand sources of understandings and misunderstandings. The notion of contexts of meaning grows from a social constructivist theory known as the Coordinated Management of Meaning theory (CMM). We provide a more complete discussion of CMM later, with emphasis on the role of contexts in meaning management.

In what follows, we will highlight the complex, intertwined dialectic that involves both "process" and "content" tensions inherent in interfaith dialogue, framing this as a tension between "grace" and "truth." We then review CMM assumptions about dialogue before introducing communicative practices that flow from these assumptions.

Grace and Truth

As authors with a shared Christian heritage, a primary scriptural text we both grew up hearing is the phrase "grace and truth." In the Christian scriptures, the first chapter in the Gospel of John states, "The Word became flesh and made his dwelling among us. We have seen his glory, the glory of the one and only Son, who came from the Father, full of grace and truth" (John 1:14). This text, when interpreted within the context of orthodox Christian thought, equates grace and truth with the historic, incarnate, and resurrected Jesus of Nazareth. We acknowledge that such a text may seem a peculiar and perhaps even divisive place to begin in examining dialogue across Abrahamic faith traditions, yet we begin here for a reason. We view this text as representing the paradoxes and dilemmas that need to be embraced for authentic interfaith dialogue. And in the spirit of authenticity, we offer insight into our individual faith journeys as needed context for understanding these paradoxes and dilemmas.

We grew up influenced by various traditions in the Christian faith. John has actively associated with and participated in a wide array of Christian faith traditions, including Roman Catholic, Baptist, Foursquare, independent, and Lutheran. Gerald was raised in the traditions of the Methodist church but has also spent time in Churches of Christ and in non-denominational, evangelical traditions. We both continue today as active members in our Christian faith communities. Furthermore, we both seek to integrate faith into our teaching, research, and service. We both welcome opportunities to engage our students in discussions about interfaith dialogue. John has organized, facilitated, and participated in conference panels focused on faith issues in university teaching and continues to critically examine metaphors of collective action reflected in contemporary evangelical Christianity.[9] Gerald applies communication theory to explore modern day church cooperation/unity movements and for years has been an active participant in one such movement in central Arkansas called the Nehemiah Network.[10]

Our twenty-five year friendship has also involved dialogue related to our efforts to engage in interfaith dialogue with others. The writing of this chapter, then, is one effort to bring together over two decades of relationship and discussions. The phrase "grace and truth" captures something of the complexity of these discussions and merits exploration at several levels: (a) as a dialectical dilemma within dialogue, (b) as a paradoxical identity, and (c) as a dialogic ideal found in each of the Abrahamic traditions.

— *Dilemma* —

At one level grace and truth represent a dialectical dilemma. We see grace as referring to a virtue that when enacted involves an unconditional respect and acceptance of the other. From the perspective of the one acting in grace, this respect and acceptance may even be seen as undeserved, which creates its own sort of dialectical tensions (i.e., this person does not "deserve" respect and acceptance, yet I am called to offer it). Those tensions are greatly exacerbated with the imperative felt by many faithful to also attend to truth and/or assert truth. While the three main Abrahamic traditions share a great deal of common ground, they also have different conceptions of truth. Many Muslims, Jews, and Christians see orthodoxy as including the embracing of some truth claims that are understood to be foundational, indisputable, universal, and by extension exclusivist.

These differing conceptions of truth confront notions of relativism. For many, a simple focus on common ground as an approach to interfaith dialogue is insufficient and ultimately promotes a monologic stance that ignores and marginalizes what may be seen as an essential element of one's faith identity. Keaton and Soukup advance what they call a "pluralistic" approach as a way to avoid the pitfalls of relativism, exclusivism, and reductionism. Yet, even in their pluralistic approach, they assume each "tradition has its 'good news' to offer."[11] However, the grace-truth dialectic recognizes that individuals representing a given faith may take the position that the faith they hold is *the* good news and that the *Truth* in their faith supersedes and, in at least some ways, refutes all others. In such cases, the good news of one faith tradition may be anything but that for another. Thus, to enact grace and truth in authentic dialogue, we must somehow confront and then both transcend and transform this dialectic dilemma.

— *Paradox* —

This dialectic, however, additionally creates a paradox of identity. As has been indicated, for many faithful what is seen as fundamental truth claims can be interpreted in terms of exclusivity. Directly following the quote from the Gospel of John already noted are these words:

> For the law was given through Moses; grace and truth came through Jesus Christ. No one has ever seen God, but the one and only Son, who is himself God and is in closest relationship with the Father, has made him known.

Orthodox Christianity is largely grounded in the teaching that in the person of Jesus people have access to truth and grace found in a relationship with the living Christ, God made flesh. The oft divisive claim that flows from this teaching is found later in the Gospel of John in which Jesus states, "I am the way and the truth and the life. No one comes to the Father except through me." The conflict is evident. The Jewish tradition rejects this claim about Jesus, as does the Islamic tradition. These phrases from Christian scripture have historically been cause for debate and division, sometimes even within Christianity. Yet the text, if taken to mean that Jesus offers something necessary and unique, implies that a Christian cannot simply *give* grace. For many faithful Christians, these teachings and many others indicate the need to share *truth*: the truth that Jesus is not a myth, nor simply a notable mystic, prophet, or teacher. The point here is clear: the identity of Christ at one level creates an impasse. As practicing Christians, both authors of this chapter recognize and at times have personally bumped up against this impasse, and we wonder: *How can the Christian live out these texts and maintain authentic dialogue, avoiding the monologic pull grounded in the covert goal or hope to convert the Jew or Muslim to the "right" understanding of Jesus?*

In fact, part of our identity as followers of Jesus involves being about grace and truth, hoping to share both, looking for and creating opportunity for dialogue. Thus, neither of us views the exclusivity of Christian truth claims—or exclusivity inherent in the truth claims of any faith tradition for that matter—as a call not to listen to others or to avoid authentic dialogue. We see that there is an *exclusive inclusivity* and, conversely, an *inclusive exclusivity* to this faith.[12] Put differently, we are committed to the possibility of avoiding both of the following: (1) viewing the identity claims about Jesus as claims intended to draw lines necessitating those who are in a particular "Jesus camp" to go out to bring others into their exclusive camp, and (2) viewing the differences across Abrahamic traditions regarding claims of Christ as claims that can be reconciled with a universalism in which all paths are understood as leading to the same goal.

There is more. Both authors understand our faith as a call to live in peace, humility, and gentleness with others. At the same time, we accept a promise of Christ (e.g., Matthew 10:34, John 15:18-20) that what we live and teach will bring division and conflict. Thus, as Christians we seek to live out this paradoxical dialogic tension; in fact, we see our very identity as demanding such effort. We believe that many faithful in all three Abrahamic traditions share this commitment and that the inherent tensions related to grace and truth, if managed well, go far in enriching interfaith dialogue.

— *Ideal* —

Finally, we find that the dialogic tension of grace and truth is also presented as a kind of prescriptive ideal in various authoritative texts of the Abrahamic faith traditions. In all three cases, particular teachings reflect on the *what* (content/truth) and on the *how* (process/grace) of communication with the other. Several key ideas grounded in Christian scripture have already been noted. For the following section, we relied on contact with individuals associated with Judaism and Islam in our relational network who shared with us texts they found relevant to the notions of grace and truth as we are exploring them here.

The Qur'an is rich with statements concerning communication, often focusing on communicating with non-Muslims. The following Qur'an excerpts reflect a concern for speaking truth, at the same time acknowledging that the way one speaks, the how of communication, is also an important issue:

- And cover not Truth with falsehood, nor conceal the Truth when ye know (what it is) (Al-Baqara 2:42).
- And be moderate in the pace, and lower thy voice; for the harshest of sounds without doubt is the braying of the ass (Luqman 31:19).
- Invite (all) to the way of thy Lord with wisdom and beautiful preaching; and argue with them in ways that are best and most gracious; for thy Lord knoweth best, who have strayed from His path, and who receive guidance (An-Nahl 16:125).
- And swell not thy cheek (for pride) at men, nor walk in insolence through the earth; for God loveth not any arrogant boaster (Luqman 31:18).
- But speak to him mildly; perchance he may take warning or fear (God) (Ta Ha 20:44).

Identifying a clear set of truth claims upon which the Jewish faith is based and which Jewish faithful feel compelled to share and defend is much more problematic. As noted on the Israel Ministry of Foreign Affairs website:

> Unlike some religions, Judaism does not believe that other peoples must adopt its own religious beliefs and practices in order to be redeemed. It is by deeds, not creed, that the world is judged; the righteous of all nations have a share in the "world to come." For this reason, Judaism is not an active missionary religion.[13]

Even though more focused on orthopraxy than on orthodoxy, Judaism does embrace both implicitly and explicitly some fundamental nonnegotiables that would certainly conflict with other belief systems, including Islam and Christianity. For example, Maimonides, a medieval philosopher, is credited with what is considered the most widely recognized and accepted of all Jewish creeds. His thirteen articles include affirming the existence and eternal nature of God, affirmations unlikely to provoke the faithful Muslim or Christian. However, his seventh article, the preeminence of Moses (rather than Muhammad) among all prophets, or his twelfth article, the future (rather than past) coming (rather than second coming) of the Messiah, are foundational claims that are not easily framed as "essentially the same thing" for that same faithful Muslim or Christian.

As for the importance of "grace" in dialogue, it has been pointed out that Judaism does not want for dictates on the subject.

> Judaism is intensely aware of the power of speech and of the harm that can be done through speech. The rabbis note that the universe itself was created through speech. Of the 43 sins enumerated in the Al Cheit confession recited on Yom Kippur, 11 are sins committed through speech. The Talmud tells that the tongue is an instrument so dangerous that it must be kept hidden from view, behind two protective walls (the mouth and teeth) to prevent its misuse.[14]

In summary, all three Abrahamic faith traditions can be understood as embodying the dialectic tension of grace and truth as related to the process and content of interfaith dialogue. For many faithful, this tension inevitably results in communicative dilemmas and paradoxes not easily assuaged with calls to let go of absolutist positions. These challenges resonate with Keaton and Soukup and their focus on the need to attend to different epistemologies. They observe:

For enormous numbers of people in the world, core ontological and epistemological beliefs are viewed as far from fluid, co-constructed, or contingent—these core beliefs are, for lack of a better term, a matter of devout faith. Ethically, communication scholars should consider our orientation to this devout faith. By embracing postmodern assumptions, we may be suggesting that devout faith (i.e., faith in a "capital T" Truth) is not valued within our theoretical understandings of dialogue. This may place communication scholars on slippery moral ground if, potentially, we are imposing our subjective postmodern or relativistic worldview upon others.[15]

Thus, we need to give attention to communicative strategies and resources that attend to this potential pitfall. Such resources must aid us in transcending the universalism relativistic dialectic that is intertwined with the grace-truth tension.

CMM: A Practical Theory to Enhance Dialogue

The Coordinated Management of Meaning first surfaced in the communication literature in the late 1970s. CMM is the work of Barnett Pearce and Vernon Cronen, and shares philosophical roots with social constructivist approaches. The intent of the theory is inspired by what Wittgenstein calls "aspect-seeing" or "noticing an aspect."[16] This type of seeing refers to the experience of seeing an object and then suddenly noticing the way it is similar or different from another object. In short, CMM aims to be a practical theory that provides a way to improve our lives, our ability to see self and other, and in the process see how our communication can be used to improve our social worlds. In this section, we first highlight the CMM theory and research tradition as a way to set up a discussion of their assumptions about dialogic communication. We then synthesize dialogic principles for application in the interfaith setting.

Barge and Pearce claim that CMM "concepts and models . . . are sensible (in the sense that they track onto empirical evidence) and useful (in the sense that they help us know how to go forward together in action)."[17] One useful CMM model is the hierarchy of meaning[18] which provides conceptualization and terminology to help understand ways in which people rely on embedded sets of interpretive contexts/frameworks to make sense of their social worlds. Concerning the ability to use CMM to track empirical data, Driskill[19] (see also Driskill and Downs[20]) found that participants in a bi-cultural organization held differing levels of awareness of the degree to which culture, episode, and relationship served as operational interpretive contexts of meaning management. In this case, participants viewed supervisor communication as less than competent without realizing the influence of culture as a context for how they were evaluating the interaction. The CMM model allowed a means for bringing greater meaning management awareness, and therefore greater interpretive latitude, to the situations, providing those involved more empowerment and option in satisfactorily managing their social environment.

CMM does more than provide interpretive insights. Beginning in the 1980s, the scope of CMM moved from interpersonal and organizational contexts to include mediation and public dialogue projects.[21] These projects foreground CMM as a practical theory, one that aids us in moving forward in action cooperatively, ethically, effectively.[22] Pearce and Pearce reflect on the process of training hundreds of individuals in facilitating public dialogic communication and in so doing capture the key learning goal of these trainings as a turning point when participants put together two concepts: "the communication perspective, which focuses on communication itself, and the characteristics of dialogic communication, as the specific, desired quality of communication."[23]

In various writings, CMM theorists provide assumptions guiding practice of the theory. We found that these assumptions are best understood first in terms of communication in general and then in terms of dialogue in particular. Pearce and Pearce posit that a communication perspective on dialogue involves three assumptions: (a) nations, organizations, families, and individuals are "deeply textured clusters of persons-in-conversation"; (b) communication itself is "substantial and its properties have consequences"; and (c) beliefs, personalities, social and economic structures should be treated as constituted in patterns of interaction—"as made, not found."[24]

Pearce and Pearce also summarize core assumptions about dialogue that inform CMM practices:

(a) Dialogue is a form of communication with specific "rules" that distinguish it from other forms. (b) Among the effects of these rules are communication patterns that enable people to speak so that others can and will listen, and to listen so others can and will speak. (c) Participating in this form of communication requires a set of abilities, the most important of which is remaining in the tension between holding your own perspective, being profoundly open to others who are unlike you, and enabling other to act similarly. (d) These abilities are learnable, teachable, and contagious. (e) There are at least three levels of these abilities, including the abilities to respond to another's invitation to engage in dialogue, to extend an invitation to another to engage in a dialogue, and to construct contexts that are conducive to dialogue. (f) Skilled facilitators can construct contexts sufficiently conducive to dialogue so that participants are enabled to engage in dialogue in ways they would not without the work of the facilitator.[25]

These assumptions echo ideals established by dialogic theory powerhouses such as Buber and Rogers and currently promoted across disciplines.[26] These ideals are also foundational to Keaton and Soukup's pluralistic approach introduced earlier.[27] Thus, as we have suggested, a paradox exists when strategies for engaging "the other" in interfaith dialogue result in unrecognized bias against anyone who cannot embrace a postmodern assumption of truth. Put differently, if someone seeking to represent their Abrahamic tradition holds a representational view of faith, the dialogue process at one level seems to call such persons to suspend belief.

We believe there are ways to apply CMM concepts to transcend this paradox. A constitutive view of communication does not negate a search for truth; put differently, there can be an allowance for meta-narratives. CMM is primarily interested in forms of communication, in what we are making with our communication. Yet, as Barnett Pearce has noted, such a view does not assume relativism. The core idea is that CMM can guide participants in interfaith dialogue to be intentional about what they are seeking to create in their communication. One final caveat, however, needs to be understood. Pearce has argued strongly that CMM is not a framework for "a (monologic) plan to be strategically implemented."[28] Instead, we concur that we should strive to engage with and learn from the dialogic processes we are studying in a dialogic way. In this process, we learn as we seek to benefit others. Thus, the following set of dialogue practices aims to encourage a dialectic dialogue process.

∞∞∞∞∞∞∞∞∞∞∞∞∞∞∞∞∞∞∞∞∞∞

CMM Dialogue Practices

Many of the following practices ideally would be facilitated in the context of public dialogue, yet we believe they still have merit if and when interfaith dialogue is less public, not allowing for or necessitating a facilitator. If a facilitator is not present, however, participants must engage in an even higher level of reflexive awareness of what they are creating together, about the choices they are making.

Our goal here is to synthesize a number of CMM principles that we find most useful and elegant for enhancing interfaith dialogue: principles such as cosmopolitan communication, transcendent eloquence, public dialogue, charmed loops, and mystery.[29] We see CMM as a sort of grammar or an enriched language for facilitating dialogue. Each practice suggested here draws on that language and seeks to enhance participant abilities to walk Buber's "narrow ridge"—the tension between holding your own perspective while being profoundly open to the other. Thus, we refer to this set of practices as interfaith bridge building as reminder that dialogue involves two making an effort, involves spanning some sort of space or chasm, and inevitably involves the risk of influencing and being influenced.

— Practice 1 —
Allow Time at the Start and at Various Junctures
for Dialogue about Dialogue

We concur with CMM theorists that dialogue involves a set of challenging, learnable, and contagious interaction skills. Therefore, time spent exploring ideas about making a dialogue process a valuable one is central. Such initiating interaction brings to focus the uniqueness of the immediate context, recognizes the merits of intentional forms of communication, and helps commit participants to building the type of bridge needed. An interfaith dialogue bridge needs to be girded with growing trust and the ability to negotiate passionately held difference.

Trust building can occur here in part because of the sharing of common ground. We encourage the following questions to enrich such trust:

- What does your faith (texts) say about "talk" and "communication" with others? What implications do these texts have for our interactions?
- What do we find in these texts related to the idea of honoring both "grace" and "truth" in our interaction? What might we do in our interaction to attend to both grace and truth?

These types of questions encourage the discoveries of personal experiences and assumptions about effective dialogue. This questioning process naturally leads to other explorations.

— Practice 2 —
Explore Assumptions about Truth, Knowledge, and Being

This philosophical turn need not be abstract. The encouragement here is to avoid moving directly to intractable differences and, instead, to areas where we can pause and reflect about our common humanity. Questions we ask here might include the following:

- We both shared faith text samples. Tell me about your journey with your scriptures. When did you first learn them? Who taught you? What factors prompt you to trust these teachings?
- Might we discuss situations when we were convinced something was true? What prompted that conviction? What counted as "proof" for you?
- Many people in our faith traditions consider these "texts" as authoritative—perhaps as the "Word of God"—and as the best or primary or exclusive source for truth. Do you consider that a fair statement? What might cause either of us to change that view or adapt it?

— Practice 3 —
Develop a Language for Comparing Assumptions, Ideas, and Beliefs

A major impasse emerges when we conclude that differing assumptions are too large to explore. It is useful here to follow Pearce and Littlejohn's admonition to create a language for comparison.[31]

Such a language avoids a focus on what appears to be incomparable or incommensurate social worlds. Thus, as one possibility, Keaton and Soukup introduce a taxonomy for religious otherness.[32] They posit a four-quadrant grid defined by two dialectical dimensions: open vs. closed experiential systems and seeking similarities-acknowledging difference. The resulting quadrants include relativism (seeking similarities/open system), pluralism (acknowledging difference/open system), reductionism (seeking similarities/closed system), and exclusivism (acknowledging difference/closed system). This model is one among many options to offer a language that could be used to prompt mutual reflection on differing epistemological assumptions.

In an electronic exchange between one of us (Gerald) and a former student who is a Sunni Muslim, the Keaton and Soukup model was shared and served as a framework for extending an ongoing interfaith conversation. The following prompts accompanied the model and served as an invitation:

- How well do you think this model and language help us to understand our own and each other's assumptions?
- How would you characterize yourself in light of these categories?
- How would you characterize me in light of these categories?

In this particular example, the value of having a shared language was evident in the student's email response, which was extensive, thoughtful, self-reflective, and filled with references utilizing the model's labels. The response seemed to deal intentionally with the paradoxes and tensions we have noted (e.g., "I am confused. What am I now? I am an Exclusivist because I think Islam is the true religion; I am not Exclusivist in the sense that I don't want to convert other people to Islam just because I think Islam is true."). Most important, it clearly indicated a desire to remain in dialogue, despite these paradoxes and tension (e.g., "What I think is that all these ways are good in some ways and wrong in other ways, but combining all these, we can get into a real dialogue *process* [emphasis added] where the chances of getting into a wrong direction are very less.").

— Practice 4 —
Respond to Each Interaction as an Anecdote
(a "To-be-continued" Story)

Discussion of CMM ideas often highlights the in-process, creative nature of stories and storytelling. The point in human interaction is to allow meanings and interpretations of one another, of your relationship, and of the content of what is being shared to have a mutable, in flux quality. Consistent with this notion, we believe fixed ideas and assumptions about the other and about a given interaction stagnate and limit interfaith dialogue. The challenge is to bracket or set aside what I think I know about the other, as well as what I might think is true based on what I learn from limited interaction with the other. Instead, if I treat the relationship as a story still being told, with yet-to-explore chapters and incomplete definitions of the relationship, and if I allow that we both have unfolding identities, then there exist possibilities for richer questions and interactions.

One specific communication tactic involves inquiring and listening to various types of stories. The hope is to gain better insight to the other's past. It is also to initiate the riskier but critical business of exploring stories that have been silenced or marginalized. For instance, one might ask questions like the following:

- What experiences have you had that prompt you to hold these convictions (stories lived)?
- What stories in your/my faith tradition would you like to know more about or understand better (stories untold)?
- What stories do you sense others in my/your faith tradition embrace that tend to be hidden, with few or none willing to discuss these (untellable stories)?

These simple, exploratory questions enrich dialogue by allowing participants to allow the story of their relationship and their faith journeys to unfold.

— *Practice 5* —
Interpret and Respond to Each Speech Act to Maintain and Enrich the Dialogue

At any turn in a dialogue, the threat and promise of progress are present. A claim, a passionately stated belief, an understanding or misunderstanding can derail the process or the opposite. We concur with Rabbi Yoffie that for dialogue to move past the obvious and boring, we must be willing to explore the differences, even differences related to that which we hold passionately.[33]

The CMM notion of a "charmed loop" can be a particularly useful concept to improve interfaith dialogue. The idea is to maintain two mutually consistent contexts in a reciprocal relationship. Pearce and Pearce explain the idea in light of Buber's tension between holding one's position and being open to the other.

> [This stance] can be understood as doing the work to keep both the concepts of self ("I am holding my own position") and relationship ("We are both profoundly open to the other") in a reciprocal relationship in which neither becomes fixed as the context for the other.[34]

Such a position encourages further dialogue about dialogue. The intent is to encourage a commitment to treating all speech acts (arguing, direct questions, presenting passionate ideas, voicing disappointment in the others, etc.) as moves to maintain this balance. Suggesting particular prompts for this practice would be difficult since it is clearly a response practice, completely dependent on the other's initiating comments. But as an example, we share an experience between Gerald and the Muslim student introduced earlier. His student noted at one point in their dialogue that he believed there was "misguidance" in both Judaism and Christianity. Such a statement could easily be taken as (perhaps even intended as) a direct challenge and possibly an attempt at a monologic shift. Applying the CMM hierarchy of meaning model, when one interprets another's speech act as such, the result is a focus on management of the self as a primary interpretive context, and, in the process, creation of serious relational context tension. However, to maintain true dialogue, the statement can and should be interpreted as the other showing trust, a willingness to present the ideas candidly. Thus, a response to encourage dialogue might be, "I am glad you trust me with your ideas about other faiths. Help me understand how you define misguided?" In fact, this was the response to the student, and the dialogue moved to such considerations. This practice requires a high degree of in-the-moment awareness and intentionality and likely would not come without practice.

— Practice 6 —
Invite Explorations of Mystery as the Highest Level of Context

CMM foregrounds that all of our talk is contextualized, that meaning is co-constructed as we consciously and, more often than not, unconsciously apply various contexts for meaning management. Thus, as in the example provided earlier, self might become a primary context, and in the process, the tension with the relational context is lost. The CMM concept of mystery invites us to create something together that promises to be transcendent in nature. Mystery presupposes that faith, like culture, involves openings for uncertainty, for differing interpretations. In short, the language used to represent our faith and the language we use to discuss faith contains certainty and a certain uncertainty. Such language leaves room, then, for us to identify different meanings, new possibilities for understanding, and even "opportunities for us to escape subjugation."[35]

Pearce explores mystery in terms of "Big M" and "little m." The idea "of Big M (mystery) is the recognition of how small and lately arrived we are in the evolution of the universe, and how short-lived will be our existence." "Little m" mystery is the "recognition of the inevitable gap between our perceptions and expressions of even the most quotidian events and objects."[36] Pearce thus invites us to think of mystery as a context, the highest level of context because of the potential this context has for transforming interactions. By definition, the level of context we select to make primary is the one that will prompt our sense of "oughtness" about how to respond to the other.

For instance, in the earlier discussion related to the charmed loop, we see how individuals (Gerald and his student) could move out of constructive dialogue if the tension between the self and relational context is not maintained. If, for instance, I begin to make self the highest context, my agenda, my desire to share or even impose my ideas becomes primary, and then I am likely to interpret speech acts by the other as denying truth or as just not wanting to hear my views. In contrast, if I am willing to embrace this tension between self and relationship, I can allow the relationship context to prompt a desire to continue in efforts to listen and also remain open. Then, if I go the next step of making mystery the main context, I will look for opportunities to experience what Pearce calls "moments of grace" or instances of "kindness, beauty, and joy" that are more likely to be perceived if mystery is the highest context.[37] Such moments grow from times when I see in the world, in the other, and in what we are creating together something that transcends grace and truth.

Each of the Abrahamic faith traditions contains encouragement to maintain humility before God and in the way we interact. More than this, paradoxically, as we seek to maintain this higher context of mystery, we are able to find the contagious nature of experiencing a Presence of the One who each faith presumes is more interested in our search for truth and grace than we could ever possibly be.

Kim Pearce (personal communication, October 7, 2011) suggests questions to aid in being intentional about making mystery the highest context. In an email, she captures an interaction with Barnett, her husband:

> As we talked tonight, Barnett said that the most profound question is, "How do we give back?" He is wondering if he has given enough. And the question that I'm wondering is, "What would it look like and how would things be different if we made acts of love and compassion our highest level of context?"

The key is to be aware and intentional about mystery, the ubiquitous and serendipitous nature of grace and truth in our world. Then, it is to use the various forms of communication already introduced (dialogue about dialogic practices, exploration of philosophical assumptions, a language for comparison, questions about various stories, creating charmed loops) to invite such mystery to serve as the highest context.

◊◊◊◊◊◊◊◊◊◊◊◊◊◊◊◊◊◊◊◊◊◊◊◊◊◊◊◊◊◊◊◊◊◊

Conclusion

Dialogue continues to be held as central to peaceful coexistence in our world. Our exploration and application of CMM to interfaith dialogue sought to address the critical need to introduce a dialectic between representational and constitutive views of reality and truth. The metanarratives of the Abrahamic faiths make claims, often embedded in history and culture, about God and humankind. In dialogue with these texts and with the other, we can make decisions to honor, question, challenge, and/or ignore these claims. To be ethical, though, dialogue must not marginalize a metanarrative by default. In fact, examination of revered religious texts suggests that communicatively oppressive practices are discouraged by these traditional metanarratives. Ironically, if a postmodern metanarrative is posited as a requirement for interfaith dialogue, it too can become oppressive, silencing other metanarratives that cannot embrace its claims. To address this ethical challenge, we propose honoring the CMM notion of mystery as the highest context, recognizing that managing the grace-truth dialectic will always involve paradox.

In practice, this means that, as we engage the other across the Abrahamic traditions, we should seek to live out a dialectic between representational and constitutive communication. We should seek to listen to the other's representation of metanarratives and look to represent our own as well, all the time recognizing we are creating something together. How we communicate matters and our willingness to explore our assumptions are vitally important. A decision to enact grace and truth, virtues central to our faiths, is central to our dialogue. We offer these six CMM informed practices in the hope that they can aid us all in this process, a dialogic process calling on serious shared creative effort. In doing so, we join with adventurer and journalist Bruce Feiler, who, at the end of his ambitious travels to the historical roots of the three monotheistic religions, offered this observation: "The most surprising thing of my trip was arriving at this distance: realizing that even though God created the world, he wants each of us to re-create it."[38]

◇◇◇◇◇◇◇◇◇◇◇◇◇◇◇◇◇◇◇◇◇◇◇◇◇◇◇◇◇◇◇◇

Notes

[1]Reuel Howe, "The Miracle of Dialogue," in *The Human Dialogue: Perspectives on Communication*, eds. F. Matson and A. Montagu (New York: New York Free Press, 1967), 148.

[2]Eric Yoffie, "Why Interfaith Dialogue Doesn't Work—and What We Can Do about It," *Huffington Post*, May 29, 2011, http://www.huffingtonpost.com/rabbi-eric-h-yoffie/why-interfaith-dialogue-d_b_867221.html.

[3]Martin Buber, "Between Man and Man: The Realms," in *The Human Dialogue: Perspectives on Communication*, eds. Floyd Matson & Ashley Montagu (New York: New York Free Press, 1967), 113.

[4]W. Barnett Pearce, "Achieving Dialogue with 'The Other' in the Postmodern World," in *Beyond Agendas: New Directions in Communication Research*, ed. P. Gaunt (Westport: Greenwood, 1993), 59-74.

[5]Floyd Matson and Ashley Montagu, introduction to *The Human Dialogue: Perspectives on Communication*, eds. Floyd Matson and Ashley Montagu (New York: New York Free Press, 1967); John Stewart and Karen Zedekar, "Dialogue as Tensional, Ethical Practice," *Southern Communication Journal* 65 (2000): 224-43.

[6]Jeffrey Murray, "Bakhtinian Answerability and Levinasian Responsibility," *Southern Communication Journal* 65 (2000): 149.

[7]Gerald Driskill, Jon Meyer, and Julien Mirivel, "Managing Dialects to Make a Difference: Tension Management in a Community Building Organization," *Communication Studies* (forthcoming).

[8]John Gribas, "Physician Heal Thyself: Tasking Student Groups with Finding Solutions to the Challenges of Communicating across Belief Systems on Campus" (presentation, Annual Meeting of the National Communication Association, Chicago, IL, November 2007).

[9]John Gribas, "Inviting Student Religious Experience into the Classroom: Benefits of Learning to Walk a Delicate Line" (presentation, Annual Meeting of the National Communication Association, San Antonio, TX, November 2006); Gribas, *supra* note 8; John Gribas, "Doing Teams While Being the Body: Managing Spiritual/Secular Dialectical Tensions of Defining the Church Collective through Transcendent Metaphor," *Journal of Communication and Religion* 31 (2008): 206-44.

[10]Gerald Driskill and Jonathan W. Camp, "The Nehemiah Project: A Case Study of the Unity Movement among Christian Church Organizations in Central Arkansas," *Journal of Communication and Religion* 29 (2006): 445-83; Gerald Driskill et al., *supra* note 7.

[11]James Keaton and Charles Soukup, "Dialogue and Religious Otherness: Toward a Model of Pluralistic Interfaith Dialogue," *Journal of International and Intercultural Communication* 2 (2009): 183.

[12]Rob Bell, *Love Wins: A Book About Heaven, Hell, and the Fate of Every Person Who Ever Lived* (New York: Harper Collins, 2011).

[13]"About the Jewish Religion," *Israel Ministry of Foreign Affairs*, http://www.mfa.gov.il/MFA/Facts+About+Israel/Spotlight+on+Israel/About+the+Jewish+Religion.htm.

[14]"Speech and Lashon Ha-Ra," *Judaism 101*, http://www.jewfaq.org/speech.htm.

[15]Keaton and Soukup, *supra* note 11 at 184.

[16]Ludwig Wittgenstein, *Philosophical Investigations* (Oxford: Blackwell, 1953), xi, 204.

[17]J. Kevin Barge and W. Barnett Pearce, "A Reconnaissance of CMM Research," *Human Systems: The Journal of Systemic Consultation and Management* 15 (2004): 13.

[18]W. Barnett Pearce and Vernon Cronen, *Communication, Action, and Meaning: The Creation of Social Realities* (New York: Praeger, 1980).

[19]Gerald Driskill, "Managing Cultural Differences: A Rules Analysis in a Bi-cultural Organization," *Howard Journal of Communication* 5 (1995): 353-79.

[20]Gerald Driskill and Cal Downs, "Hidden Differences in Competent Communication: A Case Study of an Organization with Euro-Americans and First Generation Immigrants from India," *International Journal of Intercultural Relations* 19 (1995): 505-22.

[21]Jonathan G. Shailor, *Empowerment in Dispute Mediation* (Westport: Praeger, 1994); Shawn Spano and Claire Calcagno, "Adapting Systemic Consultation Practices to Public Discourse: An Analysis of a Public Conflict Episode," Human Systems 7 (1996): 17-43; W. Barnett Pearce and Kimberly A. Pearce, "Extending the Theory of Coordinated Management of Meaning (CMM) through a Community Dialogue Process," *Communication Theory* 10 (2000): 405-23.

[22]J. Kevin Barge, "Articulating CMM as a Practical Theory," *Human Systems* 15 (2004).

[23]W. Barnett Pearce and Kimberly A. Pearce, "Taking a Communication Perspective on Dialogue," in *Dialogue: Theorizing Difference in Communication Studies*, eds. Rob Anderson, Leslie Baxter, and Kenneth Cissna (Thousand Oaks: Sage, 2004), 46.

[24]Ibid., 41-2.

[25]W. Barnett Pearce and Kimberly A. Pearce, "Combining Passions and Abilities: Toward Dialogic Virtuosity," *Southern Communication Journal* 65 (2000): 162.

[26]Buber, *supra* note 3 at Part Three; Carl Rogers, "The Therapeutic Relationship: Recent Theory and Research," in *The Human Dialogue: Perspectives*

on Communication, eds. Floyd Matson and Ashley Montagu (New York: New York Free Press, 1967), 246-59.

[27]Keaton and Soukup, *supra* note 11 at 182.

[28]Pearce, *supra* note 4 at 71.

[29]W. Barnett Pearce, *Communication and the Human Condition* (Carbondale: Southern Illinois University Press, 1989); W. Barnett Pearce and Stephen W. Littlejohn, *Moral Conflict: When Social Worlds Collide* (Thousand Oaks: Sage, 1997); Shawn Spano, *Public Dialogue and Participatory Democracy* (Cresskill: Hampton Press, 2001); Pearce and Pearce, *supra* note 21at 52.

[30]Martin Buber, *Between Man and Man* (New York: Routledge Classics, 2002), 218.

[31]Pearce and Littlejohn, *supra* note 27 at 213-14.

[32]Keaton and Soukup, *supra* note 11 at 175.

[33]Yoffie, *supra* note 2.

[34]Pearce and Pearce, *supra* note 23 at 173; Buber, *supra* note 3 at 173.

[35]W. Barnett Pearce, *In Making Social Worlds: A Communication Perspective* (Malden: Blackwell, 2007), 99.

[36]W. Barnett Pearce, "At Home in the Universe with Miracles and Horizons: Reflections on Personal and Social Evolution," http://pearceassociates.com/essays/documents/AtHomeintheUniversewithMiraclesandHorizonsv3-1.pdf, 34-5.

[37]Ibid., 34.

[38]Bruce Feiler, *Where God Was Born: A Journey by Land to the Roots of Religion* (New York: HarperCollins, 2005), 376.

Bibliography

"About the Jewish Religion." *Israel Ministry of Foreign Affairs*. http://www.mfa.gov.il/MFA/Facts+About+Israel/Spotlight+on+Israel/About+the+Jewish+Religion.htm.

Bahktin, Mikhail. *Speech Genres and Other Late Essays*. Translated by Gregory Rabassa. Austin: University of Texas Press, 1986.

Barge, J. Kevin. "Articulating CMM as a Practical Theory." *Human Systems: The Journal of Systemic Consultation and Management* 15 (2004): 192-203.

Barge, J. Kevin and W. Barnett Pearce. "A Reconnaissance of CMM Research." *Human Systems: The Journal of Systemic Consultation and Management* 15 (2004): 13-32.

Baxter, Leslie. "Dialogue of Relating." In *Dialogue: Theorizing Difference in Communication Studies*, edited by Rob Anderson, Leslie Baxter, and Kenneth Cissna, 107-24. Thousand Oaks: Sage, 2004.

Baxter, Leslie, and Barbara Montgomery. *Relating: Dialogues and Dialectics*. New York: Guilford, 1996.

Bell, Rob. *Love Wins: A Book about Heaven, Hell, and the Fate of Every Person Who Ever Lived*. New York: HarperCollins, 2011.

Buber, Martin. *I and Thou*. New York: Scribner, 1958.

———. "Between Man and Man: The Realms." In *The Human Dialogue: Perspectives on Communication*, edited by Floyd Matson and Ashley Montagu, 113-17. New York: New York Free Press, 1967.

———. *Between Man and Man*. New York: Routledge Classics, 2002.

Burke, Kenneth. *Language as Symbolic Action: Essays on Life, Literature, and Method*. Berkeley: University of California Press, 1996.

Driskill, Gerald. "Managing Cultural Differences: A Rules Analysis in a Bi-cultural Organization." *Howard Journal of Communication* 5 (1995): 353-79.

Driskill, Gerald, and Jonathan W. Camp. "The Nehemiah Project: A Case Study of the Unity Movement among Christian Church Organizations in Central Arkansas." *Journal of Communication and Religion* 29 (2006): 445-83.

Driskill, Gerald, and Cal Downs. "Hidden Differences in Competent Communication: A Case Study of an Organization with Euro-Americans and First Generation Immigrants from India." *International Journal of Intercultural Relations* 19 (1995): 505 22.

Driskill, Gerald, Jon Meyer, and Julien Mirivel. "Managing Dialectics to Make a Difference: Tension Management in a Community Building Organization." *Communication Studies* (forthcoming).

Feiler, Bruce. *Where God Was Born: A Journey by Land to the Roots of Religion*. New York: HarperCollins, 2005.

Gribas, John. "Inviting Student Religious Experience into the Classroom: Benefits of Learning to Walk a Delicate Line." Presentation at the Annual Meeting of the National Communication Association, San Antonio, TX, November 2006.

———. "Physician Heal Thyself: Tasking Student Groups with Finding Solutions to the Challenges of Communicating across Belief Systems on Campus." Presentation at the Annual Meeting of the National Communication Association, Chicago, IL, November 2007.

———. "Doing Teams While Being the Body: Managing Spiritual/Secular Dialectical Tensions of Defining the Church Collective through Transcendent Metaphor." *Journal of Communication and Religion* 31 (2008): 206-44.

Howe, Reuel. "The Miracle of Dialogue." In *The Human Dialogue: Perspectives on Communication*, edited by Floyd Matson and Ashley Montagu, 148-53. New York: New York Free Press, 1967.

Keaton, James, and Charles Soukup. "Dialogue and Religious Otherness: Toward a Model of Pluralistic Interfaith Dialogue." *Journal of International and Intercultural Communication* 2 (2009): 168-87.

Matson, Floyd, and Ashley Montagu. "Introduction: The Unfinished Revolution." In *The Human Dialogue: Perspectives on Communication*, edited by Floyd Matson and Ashley Montagu, 1-11. New York: New York Free Press, 1967.

Mead, George Herbert. *Mind, Self, and Society*. Chicago: The University of Chicago Press, 1934.

Murray, Jeffrey. "Bakhtinian Answerability and Levinasian Responsibility: Forging a Fuller Dialogical Communicative Ethics." *Southern Communication Journal* 65 (2000): 133-50.

Pearce, W. Barnett. *Communication and the Human Condition*. Carbondale: Southern Illinois University Press, 1989.

———. "Achieving Dialogue with 'The Other' in the Postmodern World." In *Beyond Agendas: New Directions in Communication Research*, edited by Phillip Gaunt, 59-74. Westport: Greenwood, 1993.

———. *In Making Social Worlds: A Communication Perspective*. Malden: Blackwell, 2007.

———. *At Home in the Universe with Miracles and Horizons: Reflections on Personal and Social Evolution*. 2011. http://pearceassociates.com/essays/documents/AtHomeintheUniversewithMiraclesandHorizonsv3-1.pdf

Pearce, W. Barnett, and Vernon Cronen. *Communication, Action, and Meaning: The Creation of Social Realities*. New York: Praeger, 1980.

Pearce, W. Barnett, and Stephen W. Littlejohn. *Moral Conflict: When Social Worlds Collide*. Thousand Oaks: Sage, 1997.

Pearce, W. Barnett, and Kimberly A. Pearce. "Extending the Theory of Coordinated Management of Meaning (CMM) through a Community Dialogue Process." *Communication Theory* 10 (2000): 405-23.

———. "Combining Passions and Abilities: Toward Dialogic Virtuosity." *Southern Communication Journal* 65 (2000): 160-75.

———. "Taking a Communication Perspective on Dialogue." In *Dialogue: Theorizing Difference in Communication Studies*, edited by Rob Anderson, Leslie Baxter, and Kenneth Cissna, 39-56. Thousand Oaks: Sage, 2004.

Rogers, Carl. "The Therapeutic Relationship: Recent Theory and Research." In *The Human Dialogue: Perspectives on Communication*, edited by Floyd Matson and Ashley Montagu, 246-59. New York: New York Free Press, 1967.

Shailor, Jonathan G. *Empowerment in Dispute Mediation*. Westport: Praeger, 1994.

Spano, Shawn. *Public Dialogue and Participatory Democracy*. Cresskill: Hampton Press, 2001.

Spano, Shawn, and Claire Calcagno. "Adapting Systemic Consultation Practices to Public Discourse: An Analysis of a Public Conflict Episode." *Human Systems: The Journal of Systemic Consultation and Management* 7 (1996): 17-43.

"Speech and Lashon Ha-Ra." *Judaism 101.* http://www.jewfaq.org/speech.htm.

Stewart, John, and Karen Zedekar. "Dialogue as Tensional, Ethical Practice." *Southern Communication Journal* 65 (2000): 224-43.

Wittgenstein, Ludwig. *Philosophical Investigations.* Oxford: Blackwell, 1953.

Yoffie, Eric. "Why Interfaith Dialogue Doesn't Work—and What We Can Do about It." *Huffington Post.* Last modified May 29, 2011. http://www.huffingtonpost.com/rabbi-eric-h-yoffie/why-interfaith-dialogue-d_b_867221.html.

Chapter 3

RELIGIOUS LITERACY AND EPCOT INTERFAITH DIALOGUE

Jacob Stutzman

While she was in seminary, my wife took a short-term class on the Holocaust and art. The class was composed of seminarians, all Protestants and mostly from mainline denominations. One of the class activities was to attend Shabbat services at one of the local synagogues. The class met at the synagogue, and all sat together through the series of services on what was an otherwise typical Saturday morning. Outside of acknowledging the visitors during the normal announcement time, the rabbi and cantor did not change their service from what they would have normally done. After services, the students had a chance to talk with the rabbi, the cantor, and the instructor, to ask questions about what they had participated in. The service had been an authentic and complete Jewish experience. The visitors were able to see the reverence with which the Torah scrolls were treated during the service, the retention of Hebrew in worship, and the requirement of communal practice in Judaism.

In many ways, that Shabbat service was an ideal interfaith experience. Well-informed believers from another faith community were able to take part in an authentic and thorough event with no expectation or obligation beyond that event. Because they were well-informed, the visitors were able to understand the proceedings, at least in part, through the lens of their own faith tradition, in much the same way that studying a foreign language often sheds light on the grammar of one's native tongue.

By contrast, a Jewish family friend became concerned that her son's public school classes had Christmas parties but did not have any Jewish representation. With the permission of her son's teacher and the principal, she came into the class one day to talk about Hanukkah. After telling an abridged version of the story and explaining the candle-lighting, she passed out small plastic dreidels to all of the students in the class. In all, she was in the room for fifteen minutes. This was, in no uncertain terms, a shallow interfaith experience. There was no reason to think these students had any idea of what it meant to be Jewish, except that it apparently meant substituting "this Hanukkah thing" for Christmas. The dreidels were nice, but they said nothing about what it meant to be Jewish or the comparison between Judaism and Christianity.

To be sure, a short and simple experience may have been the perfect approach for a class of elementary-aged children. Unfortunately, this is the same model that describes all too many adult interfaith experiences as well. What is the difference between my wife's visit to the synagogue and our friend's visit to a third-grade classroom? Why do the third-grade models of interfaith dialogue persist? I contend that one of the root causes of shallow interfaith dialogue is religious illiteracy. People simply do not know enough about religion, often including their own professed faith, to engage in meaningful interfaith dialogue.

Religious literacy, and illiteracy, is a relatively simple concept to understand. Stephen Prothero's 2007 book, *Religious Literacy: What Every American Needs to Know—and Doesn't*, made an effective case for the necessity of religious literacy to citizenship in the United States. Whether one believes or not does not much matter given the thorough intertwining of religion and civic life; religious literacy is necessary to participation in the public dialogue.[1] Taking a graduate class on Old English, I saw how the lack of religious literacy might lead one astray. We had been assigned the first ten verses of Genesis 22 to translate for the next class meeting. This portion of scripture tells the story of God testing Abraham's faith by commanding that he sacrifice his son Isaac. Those familiar with the story know that God intervenes and spares Isaac once he sees that Abraham's faith is strong. Unfortunately, that intervention does not come until the eleventh verse. One student who self-identified as an atheist came to the next class fuming at the barbarism of a deity who would ask a man to sacrifice his son. Having never before read the story, and with our assignment ending before the denouement, her reaction was understandable.

Surprisingly, a recent national study suggests that, as an atheist, my fellow student could have been expected to be more knowledgeable about the faith she was criticizing. The results of the September 2010 Pew Forum on Religion & Public Life US Religious Knowledge Survey of 3,412 adults showed that, of the 32 questions asked of participants, Protestant Christians averaged 16 correct answers and Catholics averaged fewer than 15 correct answers. Overall, the best performing groups were the agnostics and atheists (as a single group, 20.9 correct answers), Jews (20.5 correct answers), and Mormons (20.3 correct answers). In short, the Pew study results indicate that the average atheist appears to know more about religion than the average religious adherent.

The results are more telling when restricted just to the 12 questions about Christianity. While Christians overall averaged 6.2 correct answers, the only Christian subgroup to average better than 6 was white evangelicals. Otherwise, Mormons, atheists and agnostics, and Jews outperformed all Protestant and Catholic groups. So, not only does the average atheist know more than the average Christian about religion in general, but the average atheist also arguably knows more about Christianity![2]

These results are indicative of the problem of religious illiteracy and the barriers it presents to interfaith dialogue. Uninformed believers are less able to engage with interfaith dialogue partners by providing meaningful interfaith experiences or by critically participating in such experiences. Interfaith dialogue under these conditions is weakened, and a given religious tradition is presented as a pale imitation of itself. The results are shallow, albeit sometimes meaningful, experiences that I call "Epcot interfaith."

The idea of "Epcot interfaith" is simple to grasp, though it may sometimes be difficult to recognize in practice. The Epcot theme park at Walt Disney World includes the World Showcase where visitors can eat and shop in eleven country-themed pavilions staffed by citizens of the represented countries. Visiting "The American Adventure" pavilion helps to illustrate the relative shallowness of the displays. A single building, designed in the large colonial style, houses the American Adventure animatronic show, a gift shop, and a restaurant. The restaurant features, along with other "all-American" fare, barbeque. Whether the barbeque is mesquite-smoked beef in the Texas style, sweet-sauced in the Kansas City style, the vinegary-sauced pork of the Carolinas, or dry-rubbed Memphis ribs is not clear. The reductive approach to barbeque aside, where are the other American cuisines like the Tex-Mex of the Southwest, Chicago-style pizza, Maine lobster boils, Hawaiian poi and passion fruit, and fried anything-you-can-put-on-a-stick? Where are the architectural styles like the ranch homes of the Midwest, the modernist glass skyscrapers, the Mediterranean renaissance of the West Coast, or the shotgun homes of the South? Little is required to see that the American Adventure presents only the smallest slice of the United States, in a simply packaged and easily commercialized narrative.

There is something suspicious about the way the pavilions at Epcot are named though. One visits "The American Adventure," which is between "Italy Pavilion" and "Japan Pavilion." No other country is an "adventure" or an "experience," and there is no reason to think that the others are any more comprehensive national displays than the attempt at America. Such a simple experience is understandable. After all, both space and time are limited; every variation presented would lead some partisan to ask where their personal experience is in the pavilion. (Does not the Hawaiian luau meet the definition of barbeque?) And, after all, the park exists to make money. While a visit to the China Pavilion at Epcot is a better introduction to Chinese culture than no visit at all, it can hardly be considered an authentic or meaningful intercultural experience.

Unfortunately, many interfaith experiences work at the same basic level as the Epcot exhibits: come in, see some costumes, meet someone who is in the community, eat something, get a trinket, and go back to your own comfortable existence. While these interfaith experiences are also better than nothing, they are not terribly valuable. They tend to ignore varieties of experience within faith communities or meaningful comparisons between communities, and when such comparisons are made, they usually focus on difference and otherness. These sorts of events teach outsiders very little about the history or values of a religion, and they teach even less about the people who adhere to that faith. Given the prevalence of Epcot interfaith experiences, we should not be any more surprised that 62 percent of respondents to the Pew survey did not know that Vishnu and Shiva are central figures in Hinduism (as opposed to Islam or Taoism) or that only 8 percent could correctly identify Maimonides as a Jew. We would be no more surprised if someone leaving a teppanyaki restaurant could not point to Tokyo on a map.

Of course, the simple facts of a religion are not sufficient to guarantee meaningful dialogue. Eugene Gallagher argues that, in addition to basic facts, a conception of religious literacy must include "insight into how people use that basic information to orient themselves in the world, express their individual and communal self-understanding, and give their lives direction and meaning."[3] Surely such a goal is laudable, but it seems to be a more advanced step than religious literacy itself. Gallagher's goal actually seems to be the same as the goal for meaningful interfaith dialogue. The prerequisite to that dialogue, however, is the basic information of religious belief.

Two explanations are likely behind the religious illiteracy in this country. First, because of the sheer size of the Christian population in this country, it is easy to identify as a Christian. There are any number of churches to pick from, and it is a very easy trip to another church if the first one is not to your liking. Holidays are easy to manage because work and school schedules account for the major events already.[4] Supportive radio and television programming are abundant. In its broadest construction, the Christian tent is an easy one to slip into.

The accumulation of these small easements results in Christian privilege, something obviously not enjoyed by members of other religious groups. Such privilege includes the ability to ignore the perspectives of other religions and to "remain oblivious to the language and customs of other religious groups without feeling any penalty for such a lack of interest and/or knowledge."[5] The Pew study helps to reinforce this stereotype; Christians need not study other religions because Christianity is such a dominant force in American culture. As a result, only 54 percent of respondents were able to identify the Qur'an as the Muslim holy book in 2010.

The corollary is that Christians do not need to study Christianity either. A Muslim student may need to explain to a professor the custom of fasting during Ramadan, thus excusing in-class inattentiveness or difficulty. A Jewish shopper may scrutinize the labels of grocery products looking for the hechsher[6] to ensure that food he brings home adheres to Jewish dietary laws. On the other hand, Christian privileges include the assumptions that one would not have to go to work or school on holidays and that one could easily find acceptable food at stores and restaurants. There is, therefore, no cultural obligation to be educated in one's own faith the way there is for members of various religious minorities. Jewish children have to learn how to be Jewish in a primarily Christian culture and how to remain observant of the practices that set them apart. Christians need only identify as Christians. Few people will ask what it means to identify as a Christian, and almost nothing needs to be done to accommodate oneself to the world as a Christian. Once one is baptized and/or through the confirmation class at one's church, there is often little additional obligation to education.

As a freshman in college, I spent a night engaged with a friend in the sort of conversation one can only have as a first-year college student. My friend was an avowed Christian who wore her faith on her sleeve. She consciously expressed her identity as a Christian and sought out Christian people and organizations to associate with. As we talked, I mentioned the theological approach to baptism as the symbolic cleansing of original sin. My friend, the only one in the room who had been baptized, had never heard of this interpretation. In fact, she had never heard of baptism being given any theological import at all. Baptism was just something that was done, and there was no particular reason why. She was troubled by her lack of symbolic understanding of a sacrament in which she had participated compared to my understanding (which was without nuance but still more complete than hers and without the benefit of any formal Christian education). The disparity challenged her faith; how could she follow a belief system about which a nonbeliever knew more than she did?

To be clear, this does not mean that Christians do not study Christianity or that Christians do not study other religions. Obviously, many do, and this book should stand as some evidence of that. There is, however, no obligation to study and certainly not in any systematic fashion. That lack of obligation clearly manifests itself in a lack of motivation as the Pew study helps confirm that Christians do not study religion. If the systematic or thorough study of one's own faith is something generally avoided, then deep discussion of other faiths is obviously unappealing. Because of this aversion, American Christians would naturally gravitate toward shallow interfaith engagements, and those experiences would come to predominate.

The second explanation for religious illiteracy in America approaches the lack of knowledge from the other direction. Namely, if Christians are not knowledgeable about their own faith, then they will be unable to support their side of a nuanced interfaith discussion. By and large, Christians know less about Christianity than Jews and atheists know about Christianity. In that situation, it becomes impossible to have a discussion about religion that goes beyond the basic historical facts and the simplest, least-nuanced doctrinal teachings. If Christians do not know much about their own faith, how can they be expected to engage with non-Christians in meaningful interfaith dialogue? More to the point, if most Christians know only a small number of basic facts about their faith, how can Jews and Muslims and Hindus present an interfaith syllabus that goes any further into their faiths? Because many Christians cannot support their side of the conversation, the conversation is bound to reach a very quick end.

The problem of religious illiteracy, in my experience, is spreading beyond the Christian majority to include religious minorities too, and for essentially the same reasons. If Christian religious illiteracy is due in part to the ease with which a Christian identity can be adopted, then it stands to reason that as religious minorities find their identities easier to adopt and maintain, they too will fall victim to religious illiteracy. Historically, Jews were considered a "racialized other" within American culture. From the middle of the twentieth century forward though, tolerance of antisemitism dropped off, and Jews were more comfortable and more welcome to participate in broader society.[7] As the stigma that came with a Jewish identity fell away, it became easier to be Jewish. Thus the motivation for Jewish religious literacy was diminished.

The evidence suggests that religious illiteracy is on the rise in the American Jewish community. Comparing the 2000-01 National Jewish Population Survey [NJPS] with the 1971 edition of the same study shows a notable difference in regular observance of holidays and rituals. In 1971, 83.4 percent of American Jews reported observing the Passover Seder, while that number had dropped to 67 percent in 2001.[8] In 1971, 25.9 percent of Jews reported keeping kosher, but only 21 percent did in 2001.[9] The 2001 survey also noted declining enrollment in part-time Jewish educational programs such as two-evening per week models.[10] While these measures are certainly not conclusive, they are proxies for the broader question of religious literacy. If a Jew does not know how to properly run a Passover Seder, then he is not likely to host one. He is also less likely to attend a meal hosted by someone else. Keeping kosher requires considerable attention to food preparation, kitchen cleaning and maintenance, food purchases (including specialty vendors), and sometimes calls for Jews to avoid food of unknown provenance. For both Seder attendance and the maintenance of kosher eating, the decline in participation could be a symptom of declining religious literacy. Certainly that decline could be caused by the drop-off in religious education. While the 2001 NJPS notes that enrollment in day schools and yeshivas is on the rise, it does not offset the decline in enrollment in less intensive programs.

The decline in Jewish literacy is supported by anecdotal evidence as well. In my own experience, I have been twice called a "real Jew" because of my participation in relatively minimal ritual observance. While a sophomore in college, I traveled home for one of the High Holidays to attend services with my family. Upon returning to school, my roommate said that a young woman had come by our room looking for me while I was gone. He had told her that I was home for a Jewish holiday, at which point she responded, "Oh, he's a *real* Jew!" As it happened, the young woman was recruiting potential members for a Jewish student group on campus, though it seems that looking for Jewish students on one of the most important holidays, 90 miles from the nearest synagogue, was not the best strategy.

A similar pattern was repeated when my wife and I attended High Holiday services for the first time near our current home in Oklahoma City. We met a woman, also relatively new to the area, who was happy to begin introducing us to the congregation. She was very friendly and called several weeks later to invite us to Shabbat dinner. When I accepted her invitation, she immediately expressed concern that her dinner might not be observant enough for me. I expressed some confusion, and she told me that since I had been keeping up with the service when we met and reciting the prayers in Hebrew, she would not want a "serious Jew" such as myself to be offended by her relatively informal celebration.

I will confess that I do not attend services nearly as often as I should, nor do I keep kosher. I am also married to a Presbyterian pastor, and I teach at a Methodist university. While I am a studious and practicing Jew, I do not consider my willingness to attend services and my ability to participate in Hebrew particularly notable markers of a "real, serious Jew." That other Jews would disagree signals a gap between Jewish identity and Jewish learning. Thus, Jewish religious illiteracy not only impacts Jewish ritual observance, but also the quality of interfaith dialogue.

One very public example of religious illiteracy comes from the 2006 publication of the book, *The Faith Club*, by an interfaith trio of women recounting their attempts at understanding Christianity, Judaism, and Islam in the wake of the September 11 attacks. The attempt was, in and of itself, laudable. The subsequent book tour and campaign to form independent faith clubs were all the more so. At the same time, one has to wonder about the depth of the original project when the Jewish author notes that she did not define herself as a Jew.[11] When she is told that she may have additional reading to do in order to get a more comprehensive understanding of the history of the Israel-Palestine conflict, she becomes "sorry" that she shared her story with someone outside the group because she "didn't really want to read political science books about the Middle East," but wanted the interfaith experience "to be a private, personal one."[12] Indeed, more than two-thirds of the book goes by before the women share a specifically religious experience, instead spending their time in private discussion. While I have no doubt that the process described in the book was meaningful for the women who wrote it, it takes on a distinct air of intercultural rather than interfaith dialogue.

My reaction to *The Faith Club* was not unique. The authors included my home city in their tour supporting the book. In advance, my wife's church sponsored a series of discussions on the book that would focus in turn on the Christian, Jewish, and Muslim perspectives. I was asked to lead the discussion of the Jewish perspective on the book, but a fortuitous scheduling conflict combined my session with the discussion of the Muslim perspective, which was led by a local Muslim educator. She expressed the same concerns about the Muslim author as I did about the Jewish author; namely, the Muslim woman in the book did not seem to be a terribly strong example of Islam. For example, in the opening chapter of the book, the Muslim author seems unfamiliar with the story of Muhammad's night journey despite its mention in the Qur'an and its importance to a significant Muslim holiday. Moreover, as the initiator of the book project, the Muslim author says she undertook it to find reasons that her children should remain Muslim. If she could not, she "would not ask them to remain true to Islam, a religion that had come to seem to [her] to be more of a burden than a privilege in America."[13] My Muslim partner-in-dialogue was very careful not to condemn someone for doubting or studying their faith, but simply to question why someone who was in such doubt and who had studied so little should be considered a proper representative of her faith community.

Returning to my college experience, the young woman who was recruiting for a campus Jewish group was eventually successful enough to put a Hillel organization together. The group is still recognized, although their website has not been updated in over two and a half years, so I cannot speak to their ongoing level of activity. When I was still in school, this was the only organized representation of Judaism on campus. When the campus Catholic center devoted one month of their high school youth group meetings to interfaith representation, someone from Hillel was a natural choice to come and speak. As it happened, a friend of mine was working with the Catholic youth group and invited me to come as well. I appeared one Wednesday night as the third Jewish emissary alongside a Hillel member who was in the process of converting to Judaism from a mainline Protestant denomination and another Hillel member who claimed to have had a thoroughly Jewish upbringing in an observant family supplemented by a public high school with a majority-Jewish enrollment.

The proselyte student was able to make connections between Christian theology and Jewish practice in ways that I doubt I or the other Hillel representative could have made. At the same time, she was admittedly unable to answer many questions about being Jewish. That the Hillel group thought to send her at all is somewhat telling.

The other Hillel representative spent the evening demonstrating nothing more than a fundamental ignorance of Judaism and Jewish history. For example, he claimed at one point that there were thirteen tribes of Israel, the thirteenth of which was the Ashkenazi tribe. Of course, there were only twelve tribes of Israel, and Ashkenazi is a term denoting Jews of central and eastern European origin, not an ancient tribe. Given the shared literature between Catholics and Jews naming the twelve tribes of Israel, I imagine that at least a few members of the audience quickly knew that this young man was less educated in Judaism than he claimed. In the worst-case scenario, those audience members would take him to be representative of most Jews and assume that Jews do not know their own history.

More likely though, the young man's mistakes obscured one of the remaining differences in the American Jewish experience. Ashkenazi Jews worship with a liturgy distinct from that of the Sephardic (Spanish and Portuguese) Jews, and the two groups differ on some points of ritual. As would be expected with different geographical origins, there are also notable cultural differences of music and food. Additionally, there was historical conflict between the Ashkenazi Jews, as the driving organizational force behind Zionism and the state of Israel, and the Sephardic Jews they considered to be unlettered, uncultured, and backward. None of that history is accessible to an audience that believes the Ashkenazi are so-called after a descendant of Jacob. There would be no discussion of those differences, nor any indication that those differences existed. Not only did religious illiteracy hinder the potential for genuine interfaith discussion that night at the Catholic center, but it also almost surely contributed to additional confusion and obfuscation.

Was this case of religious illiteracy a function of the ease of growing up Jewish in a heavily Jewish area? Did this young man's religious education focus on ritual without the accompanying historical context? Did he simply not pay much attention to his religious education? It is impossible to say, of course, but the results were unmistakable. It is not necessary to understand the historical divisions of the twelve tribes or the difference between Ashkenazic and Sephardic practices in order to have a meaningful interfaith experience. When it is not possible to understand those histories or differences though, when they are effectively erased, then the Epcot interfaith experience has become not only the display one community puts on for the other, but also it becomes the experience a faith community constructs for itself.

Imagine if the Japan Pavilion at Epcot were not just a shallow representation of Japan to non-Japanese people, but instead became *the* experience of Japan and Japanese culture for both visitors and the Japanese. Regional culinary variations would be erased. Architecture and dress would no longer carry any sense of history or adaptation to local circumstances. Identifiable contributions from Japanese culture would be lost. Indeed, Disney did not add an anime exhibit to the Japan Pavilion until July 2010. The pavilion has no role for technological advancement or high-tech industry nor the impact that World War II had on the culture and government of Japan. If the whole of the Japanese experience were contained in the Japan Pavilion, it would hold little attraction either for Japanese people or visitors from other cultures. If the Japan Pavilion and Japan were synonymous, we would find little cultural value in either.

Religious experiences that are similarly shallow in order to cater to religiously illiterate members of the community hold a similarly low level of attraction. Whether Jewish services that eschew traditional practices because people are unfamiliar with them or Christian sermons that avoid discussing scriptural passages which require historical context to properly understand, shallow religious experiences hide the problem of religious illiteracy by lowering the bar.

From a broader cultural perspective, the loss of thorough and meaningful religious experience is a cost to everyone. Within the sphere of interfaith dialogue, the loss of religious literacy leaves fewer and fewer believers who can meaningfully participate. The consequences become clear when one considers that maintaining dialogue is the key to preventing religious conflict and effective dialogue can only be served by religiously literate partners. Without religious literacy, Epcot interfaith becomes the natural choice for those in the religious minority as they display their faith to other communities. Eventually, there is the risk that Epcot religion is all that remains. Religious literacy is essential to preventing the reduction of religion to a building, a restaurant, and a trinket. Knowing one's own faith, and evincing a willingness to continue studying it, should be a prerequisite to interfaith dialogue worthy of the name.

◇◇◇◇◇◇◇◇◇◇◇◇◇◇◇◇◇◇◇◇◇◇◇◇◇◇◇◇

Notes

[1]Stephen Prothero, *Religious Literacy: What Every American Needs to Know—and Doesn't* (HarperOne, 2007), 11-13, 39-55.

[2]"US Religious Knowledge Survey," (Washington, DC: Pew Forum on Religion & Public Life, 2010).

[3]Eugene V. Gallagher, "Teaching for Religious Literacy," *Teaching Theology & Religion* 12, no. 3 (2009): 208.

[4]Lewis Z. Schlosser and William E Sedlacek, "Religious Holidays on Campus: Policies, Problems, and Recommendations," a report published by the University of Maryland Counseling Center, (2001): 3-5.

[5]A list of accumulated Christian privileges is discussed, including the two quoted here, in Lewis Z. Schlosser, "Christian Privilege: Breaking a Sacred Taboo," *Journal of Multicultural Counseling and Development* 31, no. 1 (2003): 48-49.

[6]The hechsher is the marking applied to food packaging to certify that it is kosher. Hechshers will vary based on the various authorities that certify the food, the type of food contained in the package, and sometimes the origin of the ingredients used to make the food. Observant Jews will typically only eat food that has been certified as kosher.

[7]W. J. Blumenfeld, "Christian Privilege and the Promotion of 'Secular' and Not-So 'Secular' Mainline Christianity in Public Schooling and in the Larger Society," *Equity & Excellence in Education* 39, no. 3 (2006): 202-03.

[8]Fred Massarik, "National Jewish Population Study Highlights: Jewish Identity," (New York: Council of Jewish Federations, 1971), 11; United Jewish Communities, *The National Jewish Population Survey 2000-01: Strength, Challenge and Diversity* (New York, 2003), 7.

[9]Massarik, "National Jewish Population Study Highlights: Jewish Identity," 11; Communities, "The National Jewish Population Survey 2000-01: Strength, Challenge and Diversity," 7.

[10]———, "The National Jewish Population Survey 2000-01: Strength, Challenge and Diversity," 14-15.

[11]Ranya Idliby, Suzanne Oliver, and Priscilla Warner, *The Faith Club* (New York: The Free Press, 2006), 7.

[12]Ibid., 25.

[13]Ibid., 5.

◇◇◇◇◇◇◇◇◇◇◇◇◇◇◇◇◇◇◇◇◇◇◇◇◇◇

Bibliography

Blumenfeld, Warren J. "Christian Privilege and the Promotion of 'Secular' and Not-So 'Secular' Mainline Christianity in Public Schooling and in the Larger Society." *Equity & Excellence in Education* 39, no. 3 (2006): 195-210.

Gallagher, Eugene V. "Teaching for Religious Literacy." *Teaching Theology & Religion* 12, no. 3 (2009): 208-21.

Idliby, Ranya, Suzanne Oliver, and Priscilla Warner. *The Faith Club*. New York: The Free Press, 2006.

Massarik, Fred. "National Jewish Population Study Highlights: Jewish Identity." New York: Council of Jewish Federations, 1971.

Prothero, Stephen. *Religious Literacy: What Every American Needs to Know—and Doesn't*. New York: HarperOne, 2007.

Schlosser, Lewis Z. "Christian Privilege: Breaking a Sacred Taboo." *Journal of Multicultural Counseling and Development* 31, no. 1 (2003): 44-51.

Schlosser, Lewis Z., and William E. Sedlacek. *Religious Holidays on Campus: Policies, Problems, and Recommendations*. College Park: University of Maryland, 2001.

United Jewish Communities. *The National Jewish Population Survey 2000-01: Strength, Challenge and Diversity*. United Jewish Communities: New York, 2003.

"US Religious Knowledge Survey." Washington, DC: Pew Forum on Religion & Public Life, 2010.

Chapter 4

BUILDING BRIDGES: A PROPOSAL OF THE CHARTRAIN LABYRINTH AS PARADIGM FOR THE TRANSFORMATIONAL JOURNEY OF INTERFAITH DIALOGUE

Elizabeth McLaughlin

There will be no peace among the nations without peace among the religions.

—**Hans Kung**

It is solved by walking (solvitur ambulando).

—**Attributed to St. Augustine**

Entering Chartres Cathedral filled my soul with wonder. The classic Gothic architecture, stained glass windows, and sculpture testify to the collective faith of the individual artisans who worked anonymously to create a temple for God. Beneath it all is the labyrinth. Covered by folding chairs, it was still strikingly there—the huge prayer circle used for centuries by pilgrims walking the Road to Jerusalem, or possibly praying for hands-and-knees purification before viewing the Veil of the Virgin Mary, and perhaps reenacting the Paschal drama. The Chartrain Labyrinth, the eleven-circuit, unicircular path structured around the image of the cross, has led many individual pilgrims on a one-way path toward the center and then out again. This path represents their individual journeys of faith. Used by many cultures and religions through the centuries, the labyrinth is not a maze or a game where one can get lost, but rather it is a rich metaphor for understanding and reenacting the journey of life.[1]

When I first saw the labyrinth, I did not know any of this. *I needed a narrative to help me understand and envision the power of the symbol that lay before me.* Our tour guide told us how pilgrims would come to Chartres to see the Veil of the Virgin Mary that tradition says she wore while giving birth to Jesus. He also said that some pilgrims would crawl on their hands and knees on the path to do penance before seeing the veil. I found another labyrinth a couple of years later while at Mary's Solitude, a retreat center on the campus of St. Mary's College across from the University of Notre Dame. This outdoor labyrinth, situated in a beautiful garden, consisted of a seven-circuit pattern set in round stepping-stones. I read the plaque at the side about the steps of walking: "Letting Go," "Illumination," and "Union"—but did not "get it." Something was supposed to happen, but I did not know what.

After September 11, 2001, and the growing thunder of potential global war, there is no argument about the vital importance for people of different faiths—particularly Christians, Jews, and Muslims—to seek ways of bridging their histories and differences to try to forge a more peaceful world. While the spirit for peace may be willing, the flesh yearns for something to change, without knowing what. The voices and violence screaming for justice and retribution often seem more tangible than real actions for peace. Communication scholars must actively participate in peacemaking efforts and offer the knowledge and wisdom of our field to help find life-changing ways to bring people together.

Understanding how visual metaphors and their surrounding narratives can transform the lives of believers and inform interfaith dialogue is the heart of this chapter. Through an understanding of visual archetypes like the labyrinth, I propose that people of faith can better experience the transformational narratives of their own traditions and then use these metaphors as the vehicles for understanding the narratives and rituals of other traditions. In turn, a community can be forged to further peacemaking. To explore this premise, I proceed in three sections.

In section one, I explore key questions and models for interfaith dialogue and address the importance of both the cognitive and affective aspects necessary to achieve true understanding. Next, I explore the nature of ritual and the power of presentational symbols to facilitate dialogue employing the work of philosopher Susanne K. Langer, as participants are transformed through their ritualized participation and identification with their sacred stories. The visual archetype of the labyrinth is one example of a transformative presentational symbol that has spoken to people in many cultures and contexts.

Finally, I offer a modest proposal for use of symbols like the Chartrain Labyrinth to help structure transformational interfaith dialogue and community building that transcends the limitations of exclusivism and syncretism. It is possible for members of one tradition to listen to and understand how the sacred narratives and rituals of another faith work to transform its believers on life's journey without sacrificing the narratives that make either unique. This transformation includes the potential for deeper exploration of one's own faith journey, while appreciating and honoring the differences of others. This shared understanding can help foster peacemaking.

This inquiry raises several relevant questions for communication scholars seeking to create a greater understanding between people of all faiths to create a more peaceful world. How do visual symbols and their surrounding narratives work together to help transform people's lives? What is their potential for interfaith dialogue? How does the conception of a visual archetype change, as it is adapted from one faith tradition and applied to another faith or discipline? How does "telling our story" well through discursive and non-discursive forms influence how people live out their beliefs? Does a better understanding of one's own faith narratives—grounded in the connection of word and symbol—help a person convey this meaning to another? How can visual archetypal symbols enhance interfaith dialogue without sacrificing the unique faith narratives of a tradition? In a time when religious differences have become the rhetoric of war between nations and ideologies, these are important questions.

Interfaith Dialogue: Models, Process, and Content

What is interfaith dialogue and what are the different approaches to achieving it? To define the terms and concepts of this chapter, I am drawing basic approaches and concepts from *Unity in Diversity: Interfaith Dialogue in the Middle East,* by peace scholars Mohammed Abu-Nimer, Amal I. Khoury, and Emily Welty. These authors define dialogue as "a safe process of interaction to verbally or nonverbally exchange ideas, thoughts, questions and information, and impressions between people of different backgrounds."[2] Interfaith dialogue differs from debate about religion, which seeks to sell and persuade, "evaluate and select the best," justify, or to find only one meaning. Interfaith dialogue seeks to learn, share meaning, and examine the assumptions and perspectives of others for peacemaking.[3] The religious nature of interfaith dialogue calls for participants to engage "their deepest motivations, beliefs and fears" in the search for commonalities in the cause of peace.

These authors also offer four different approaches or attitudes that people bring to the table of interfaith dialogue: exclusivism, syncretism, pluralism, and transformative dialogue. These approaches can be viewed as a continuum of how parties perceive their own faith in relation to the faith and practices of their communication partners. The person who is exclusivist "believes that only his or her religion is fundamentally and universally true," and this approach is the "least conducive" to interfaith dialogue.[4] This approach focuses on apologetics and conversion, which runs counter to dialogue. However, the authors note that persons with this approach bring a deep understanding and knowledge of their faiths.[5]

At the other end of the spectrum is syncretism, which seeks to "merge two or more faiths into a single, unified faith."[6] While this approach might appear to be helpful, the authors contend that "religious uniformity" is not the goal of interfaith dialogue, but rather "the building of relationships."[7] In some cases, the spiritual practices of syncretism eclectically borrow the beliefs, rituals, and practices of other faiths in an attempt to support this movement toward a thin unity. To many, this can make efforts for interfaith dialogue look like an entirely new religion.[8] This approach does not honor the important differences in beliefs and worldviews of the faiths attempting to dialogue.

Pluralism, a term imbued with many meanings, is, according to these authors, considered the ideal approach from the West. In pluralism, the inherent worth of all religions is affirmed, while retaining the boundaries of one's own faith. "Parallel myths and themes" and "recognizing the validity" of others are hallmarks of pluralism.[9] While pluralism is useful in many contexts, it can also lead to a type of universalism and ignore some of the deeper differences between religions.[10]

Transformative dialogue, the interfaith dialogue model used in this chapter, in itself is a kind of religious experience as, together, its participants recognize "the increasing interdependence of a globalized world in a way other models do not."[11] In this approach, differences are honored and similarities are recognized. Sharing a deep faith offers participants common ground for appreciating the unique lens of a religious identity. "We are, in the end, defined as much by what we are not as we are defined by what we are."[12] One expectation of the transformative approach is that its participants will experience a type of conversion to a renewed version of their own faiths, while being better informed and "more compassionate towards the other party."[13] Change is expected and is a part of the transformative process. The process itself is a type of spiritual journey where each participant is purged of stereotypes about others and the flat notions of one's own faith, and then experiences illumination of reaffirmation and discovery. Finally, in the union of shared experience and a sense of mutual appreciation, group members can be changed. Once transformation for all parties is happening, the foundation for peacemaking efforts is set in place.

Abu-Nimer, Khoury, and Welty also note the importance of the subjects to be addressed during interfaith dialogue. The cognitive models "focus on the exchange of information," while the affective model "centers on building relationships and concentrates on participants' sharing stories."[14] Cognitive dialogue models do not ignore stories, but rather stress the importance of understanding each other's theology as the path to peace. The cognitive can be limiting as it does not address culture, politics, and the personal. As these peace scholars describe it, cognitive models seek to provide a more objective basis for understanding the other by understanding the belief systems and narratives of the other.

On the other hand, the affective model encourages the sharing of personal stories and how these stories relate to the larger faith narratives. This model goes beyond exchanging information to "help participants find the other within themselves."[15] The affective connects the deeper questions and mysteries of life to the narratives of faith. Through personal storytelling, the authors suggest, the cognitive and affective can be balanced as participants express their experiences and feelings with greater depth. Participants can articulate their values without debating the differences in narratives and doctrine. Differences are acknowledged within a relationship of mutual understanding and not argument about the nuances.

The Ritual Power of Presentational Symbols and the Journey of Life

Elsewhere, Mohammed Abu-Nimer argues that interfaith dialogue groups can effectively—and carefully—employ rituals and symbols as a means for opening new windows of understanding. Participants must be careful to honor the nature of each other's rituals, but can create a "third culture" of their own through the process of dialogue.[16] Rituals and symbols can include the cognitive and affective sharing of meaning between peoples of faith and can be useful in building relationships and special group identity. Archetypal symbols, which can be found in many traditions, can serve as the means for creating rituals that honor more than one tradition and structure greater understanding.

Philosopher Susanne K. Langer explains the importance of both discursive and non-discursive symbols in her work on presentational symbols like the Chartrain Labyrinth. In her books, *Philosophy in a New Key* and *Feeling and Form*, she posits that symbolism is the basis of all human knowing and understanding. In her framework, language is not merely a mode of communication, but rather symbols that construct our reality and meaning. Two types of symbols compose meaning for humans: language symbols, representing discursive modes using words, and non-discursive ritual symbols, which are presentational in nature.

According to Langer, presentational forms include music, dance, fashion, ritual, and art—symbols that convey emotional meaning and which must be considered as a whole for their proper meaning. In other words, human logic and our ability to perceive the world and share meaning are wrapped up in the unified functioning of symbols that use words and symbols that do not use words. As conveying meaning, these symbols give shape to meaning, as "feelings have definite forms, which become progressively articulated."[17] Discursive symbols in the form of language and text can give shape and context to a story, while the presentational symbol or visual image gives form to the emotional logic. I argue that the labyrinth, as a presentational form, shapes the emotive response of the walker, within the frame of the ritual shaped by its sacred narrative. Presentational symbols, then, serve to bring together the cognitive and the affective in active participatory storytelling which can transform participants.

For a presentational form to be understood and the ideas of feeling to be apprehended by an audience, Langer argues that the art must be congruent as a "gestalt" between the form and the "vital experience."[18] Abstraction, plasticity, and transparency all convey symbolic meaning for audiences.[19] While many factors are a part of these results, Langer identifies "space-tensions" and "space-resolutions" as the interplay of aspects that create community between the symbolic form and the "morphology of feeling."[20]

The understanding of religious faith as a spiritual journey where believers are pilgrims transformed by the divine is common to all faiths. The image of the pilgrim and pilgrimage is common to Islam, Judaism, and Christianity. The journey archetype or the understanding of life as a journey beginning at birth and ending at death is found in the visual symbol of the labyrinth. Describing characteristics of the spiritual journey "arising from the medieval Christian mystical experience," Michael P. Graves mentions the threefold path of Purgation, Illumination, and Union as one very significant pattern of the spiritual journey and uses Victor Turner's term "communitas" to describe "the unique fellowship of pilgrimage" that develops on the road.[21] These terms apply to understanding how the presentational symbol of the labyrinth, as a visual archetype, serves as a vehicle for transformation and interfaith dialogue.

The Labyrinth as a Visual Archetype of Life's Journey

The pattern of the maze or labyrinth is found in many times and cultures. Labyrinths and mazes reportedly go back 4,000 years and have been seen as patterns in ancient pottery and etched into stone drawings. Based on shapes found in nature, the labyrinth has been associated with Native Americans, Celts, mystical Judaism, ancient Greece, and even with energy fields and Chakras.[22] Labyrinths have appeared in illuminated manuscripts and carved into the face of hill-sides. They have been used as a symbol of protection, the focus of playing and dancing, a metaphor of the journey up a sacred mountain, and a means of controlling the weather.[23] The spiral path with one way of walking is ever ancient, ever-present, and ever new.

Labyrinths are archetypal symbols, which can mediate an understanding of unseen realities. In their article on archetypal criticism, James W. Chesebro, Dale A. Bertelsen, and Thomas F. Gencarelli identify seven features that archetypes share. These principles are found in the symbol of the labyrinth: *recurrence; analogy; human constructivism* (desire to show relationships between "diverse entities"); *conventionality* (social contracts in community); *ambiguity* ("degree of variance and unpredictability"); *epideictic understanding* ("mystery"); and *reduction* (translates "humanly created knowledge").[24] Archetypes help interpret and mediate symbolic meaning that makes the invisible visible and makes mystery applicable to human life. In whatever culture, mythology, or context where it is present, the labyrinth is analogous to the journey metaphor, expressing mystery and ambiguity while implying relationships between things and ideas and an expected social response.

Depicting the journey of life, the pilgrim or traveler begins to take the first step at birth and then meanders toward the center before coming back out. In whatever context the archetype is used, the traveler faces at the center either a monster or a trial to overcome or an illumination to take back into the world. This archetypal metaphor of the journey is central to religious discourse. Michael P. Graves names the symbol of the journey as "one of the most pervasive symbols in religious literature" and says that it is "the key central symbol in Christian mystical literature" because it "has the ability to compress and express many levels of meaning."[25]

The Labyrinth and the Journey of Interfaith Dialogue

The journey metaphor common to Abrahamic faith traditions can effectively become the locus of the third culture required by transformative interfaith dialogue—when the narratives and experiences of participants are honored and shared. However, some efforts do not respect narrative difference. In this final section, I explore how visual metaphors, specifically the labyrinth, are being used in interfaith dialogue. While no doubt these efforts are well intended, I believe that present use of the labyrinth falls into the category of syncretism that fails to acknowledge the real differences between different traditions, their stories, and practices. I offer this modest proposal that applies the ritualized use of the labyrinth to the transformative interfaith dialogue model recommended by Abu-Nimer, Khoury, and Welty, as faith communication partners interact with the journey metaphor and how it affects their stories. Their journey toward unity in the midst of diversity offers the hope for peace.

In Acts 17, the Apostle Paul demonstrates one approach to interfaith dialogue by referring to a visual symbol in his speech before the Council of the Areopagus. While seeking common ground to discuss the Christ story with the Jews, Epicureans, and Stoics of Athens, he refers to a familiar worship symbol: an altar "To an Unknown God" and then frames his discourse within this symbol (Acts 17:23). Paul proceeds to discuss his narrative interweaving the narratives of the Greek poets (Acts 17:28). As a result, his discourse was heard and measured: most laughed and some accepted it (Acts 17:32-34). Paul used a familiar visual image, understood the narratives that framed it that were different from his own, and used this image to communicate his story. However, from the point of view of interfaith dialogue, Paul's perspective was one of persuasion and conversion, reflecting an exclusivist position. While quoting the poets and texts of his audience, Paul considered his position universally true.

On the other end of the interfaith dialogue spectrum are the current uses of archetypal symbols like the labyrinth to promote interfaith dialogue in a syncretistic manner. While these efforts and practices seek to honor the stories of all faiths in the quest for peace, they do the opposite by ignoring the essential differences, narratives, and worldviews each tradition holds dear. In the words of Timothy George, dean of Beeson Divinity School, "amalgamation" is both a "distortion" that does not honor "the most essential things," and "a sign of disrespect" that "fails to take seriously what each religion claims is ultimate truth."[26]

Labyrinths are becoming increasingly popular, and many faith and spirituality traditions are adopting them to promote spiritual growth. As the number of groups using the labyrinth has increased, so has the narrative incoherency of what these practices mean. In *Walking a Sacred Path: Rediscovering the Labyrinth as a Spiritual Tool*, Lauren Artress describes her experience of walking the Labyrinth of Chartres in January 1991. As canon of Grace Cathedral in San Francisco and a psychotherapist, she was in a period of personal transition. After walking the path, she reflected on the universal need for the divine. "I began to realize the profound need we have to connect to the Spirit that enlivens us. We need that core feeling of connection to the Divine to give our lives meaning." Further, she affirms the need "to awaken to a vision of a thriving, healthy planet that supports life among diverse communities." She continues, "To evoke our vision, we need the experiences of archetypes [like the labyrinth] that help us grasp the experiences of unity and wholeness."[27]

After her encounter with the Chartrain Labyrinth, Artress reproduced two different labyrinths at Grace Cathedral, where many different groups and thousands of people have reportedly walked the path.[28] What is notably missing from this narrative is how this archetype relates to journey narratives of the Bible or any journey narratives for that matter. With vague references to the divine feminine and the journey of life, pilgrims largely bring and construct their own meanings. While this may be helpful in some contexts, this blurring and omission of narrative coherence can work against transformative interfaith dialogue.

The Labyrinth of Peace, in Brandon, California, is another example of syncretistic practice using the labyrinth without a compelling narrative to inform its practice for interfaith dialogue. Located at Brandon University, the newly opened outdoor labyrinth, built in the Chartrain pattern, features symbols from "Baha'i, Buddhism, Christianity, Daoism, Earth Religions, Hinduism, Islam, Judaism, Native Religions and Sikhism" as expressions of multiculturalism and the faith diversity of the community.[29] These symbols "represent many paths to the divine" and speak to the community's rich cultural heritage. Besides promoting awareness of the many faith traditions, the value of walking this path appears to be as a form of exercise. Without a narrative to connect with, how can people change? Without acknowledging the narratives and transformations of individual faith, how can people come together and share their uniqueness in interfaith dialogue?

◇◇◇◇◇◇◇◇◇◇◇◇◇◇◇◇◇◇◇◇◇◇◇◇◇◇◇◇◇

A Modest Proposal for Transformative Interfaith Dialogue Using the Labyrinth

I propose the following ritual sequence as a potential paradigm for transformative religious discourse. One underlying assumption is that both the cognitive and affective parts of each participant's faith must be explored, heard, and respected in order for the group to formulate and execute meaningful peacemaking efforts. This model features the labyrinth as a transformative symbol that should be comfortable for all faiths. Following the caution offered by Abu-Nimer, Khoury, and Welty against the potential dilemmas of using common prayer as a tool, I recommend, "a shared silence in which participants may choose to pray in whatever manner they are most comfortable."[30] This model follows the steps of the spiritual journey using the labyrinth and leads the group through their own journey of transformation in a formation of a third culture that honors the narratives and experiences of each member.

After the introduction of the stages of the spiritual journey—purgation, illumination, and union—each group member will individually walk the labyrinth exploring his or her faith and how it has been formed in narrative and practice. This reflection will include both the cognitive and affective aspects of the individual's faith journey. Key focus questions include "what do you know to be true about your faith and how has this understanding changed your life? How does your faith transform you into a better person? How do your sacred writings speak to your life?" After a period of shared silence, group members write down and share their experience within the group.

— *Purgation* —

Following this period of individual reflection, each person will share his or her story with group members. After this sharing of personal stories, the group members will ask clarifying questions about various parts of the story for empathic understanding. Within this step, members have the opportunity to understand their own faith and hear the stories of others. This is a step of facing and releasing illusions and accepting the realities of one's own faith, while creating sacred space to hear the stories of others. After all members have shared their stories, the group will walk the labyrinth together in the understanding that they are symbolically journeying together toward a new understanding.

— Illumination —

Following this communal walk, the step of illumination begins with questioning each other about the stories, experiences, and beliefs in the desire to displace stereotypes, let them go, and replace them with mutual respect and understanding. In this step, the goal is to broaden understanding of faith traditions as it has been lived by the other. Issues of pain and anger may emerge in this process, which must be acknowledged and heard. This step of illumination can include the acknowledgment of loss and the encouragement of healing. The process of illumination may help to forge better relationships of mutual respect and regard for what is real between group members' traditions. The necessity for confession and forgiveness may be necessary in the step of illumination and cannot be set aside or ignored. "When words fail," note Abu-Nimer, Khoury, and Welty, "rituals can often be the bridge of understanding between the gulfs of hurt or confusion that may arise in IFD."[31] Following this sharing and clarification, a process that must be given due time, group members will again walk the labyrinth together, perhaps in dyads or triads, to reinforce the growth of the light they are beginning to share.

— Union —

Finally, in the stage of union, group members individually reflect on their experience and then share these results with the group. Hopefully, members will have been changed and enriched by their transformative encounter with the group and "will behave differently after the dialogue."[32] This can include a new appreciation for their own faith and the experience of "being better informed or more compassionate toward the other party."[33] Once again, for a concluding time, participants again walk the labyrinth together in a symbol of the transformation they have experienced together. Walking again together can be a type of ritual that "can be a way of recognizing, encouraging, and celebrating the transformation that can occur in the context of dialogue."[34] This third culture of shared understanding structures the possibility of transformation in ways that honor the narrative traditions of Abrahamic faith.

While this paradigm is a sketch at best, it offers an adaptive model for interfaith dialogue that can respect differences while seeking unity. Interfaith dialogue is a complicated process that requires an active commitment and sacrifice from all members to achieve. Peace activists Abu-Nimer, Khoury, and Welty offer the following set of ground rules for constructive interfaith dialogue, and these guidelines apply to the proposed model for the labyrinth ritual previously described. Their recommendations for interfaith dialogue participants include: speak for yourself, recognize the complexity of religious traditions, hold meetings within one's own tradition first ("unireligious caucuses first"), no apologetics, resist watering down of beliefs, attend to power dynamics, suspend roles and status within the group, and establish rules within the group.[35]

Can walking the labyrinth lead to a more peaceful world? Maybe not. However, the transformative power of visual archetypes remains a largely unexplored area of research in interfaith dialogue. The journey archetype can contribute to *intra*faith and *inter*faith dialogic encounters to help us share and understand our own narratives, understand our similarities and differences better, and even as a context for understanding the narratives of others. Understanding how other faiths consider change, develop relationships, live in community, find meaning, and determine their values, may make possible more harmonious, transformative relationships.

◇◇◇◇◇◇◇◇◇◇◇◇◇◇◇◇◇◇◇◇◇◇◇◇◇◇◇◇◇◇◇◇

Conclusion

The journey archetype is found in most cultures, and the labyrinth as a visualization of life's journey transcends the differences of religious traditions. Northrop Frye in his essay on the journey metaphor argues that metaphor is the primary language and defines the journey metaphor in religious use as an emphasis on the way we are all traveling:

A journey is a directed movement in time and through space and in the idea of a journey there are always two elements involved. One is the person making the journey; the other is the road, path or direction taken, the simplest word for this being *way*. In all metaphorical uses of the journey these two elements appear. In pure metaphor, the emphasis normally falls on the person; in proportion as we approach religious and other existential aspects of metaphorical journeys the emphasis shifts to way.[36]

Because the labyrinth is a visual archetype of the journey, it serves as a presentational symbol for describing and understanding different narratives concerning the nature of the pilgrim and the pilgrimage in different faith traditions. Through an understanding of visual archetypes like the labyrinth, people of faith can better-experience the transformational narratives of their own traditions, and then work with these metaphors as bridges for understanding the narratives and rituals of other traditions. As an archetypal metaphor, the labyrinth serves as a ritual location for civil religious discourse between persons seeking to understand each other's journeys of faith. Sharing our metaphors and our lived stories enhances the universal quest for the Holy Grail of a more peaceful world. Perhaps it is solved by walking.

Notes

[1]Historian Jeff Saward connects the pattern with ancient Greece, Native Americans of Arizona, as well as Rome and Medieval Europe, in *Labyrinths: Their Mystery and Magic*, directed by Richard Feather Anderson, Jeff Saward, and Robert Ferre (Russellville, CA: VisionQuest Video, 2000), VHS.

[2]Mohammed Abu-Nimer, Amal I. Khoury, and Emily Welty, *Unity in Diversity: Interfaith Dialogue in the Middle East* (Washington: United States Institute of Peace Press, 2007), 8.

[3]Ibid.

[4]Ibid., 12.

[5]Ibid., 13.

[6]Ibid.

[7]Ibid.

[8]Ibid.

[9]Ibid., 14.

[10]Ibid., 15.

[11]Ibid.

[12]Ibid.

[13]Ibid., 16.

[14]Ibid.

[15]Ibid., 16-17.

[16]Mohammed Abu-Nimer, "The Miracles of Transformation: Are You a Believer?" in *Interfaith Dialogue and Peacebuilding*, ed. David R. Smock (Washington: United States Institute of Peace Press, 2002), 18.

[17]Susanne K. Langer, *Philosophy in a New Key* (Cambridge, MA: Harvard University Press, 1942), 94.

[18]Susanne K. Langer, *Feeling and Form* (New York: Charles Scribner's Sons, 1953), 59.

[19]Ibid., 59-60.

[20]Ibid., 370.

[21]Michael P. Graves, "Stephen Crisp's *Short History* as Spiritual Journey," *Quaker Religious Thought* 26 (1993): 6-8.

[22]On the Internet, there are a host of events, groups, therapies, religions, speakers, products, books, and articles linking to a labyrinth of many websites. One such site is The Labyrinth Society http://www.labyrinthsociety.org/. I counted at least five sites where a person could "walk" the labyrinth with a computer mouse. Of these, two sites had musical accompaniment, which, of course, could be purchased.

[23]Anderson et al., *supra* note 1.

[24]James W. Chesebro, Dale A. Bertelsen, and Thomas F. Gencarelli, "Archetypal Criticism," *Communication Education* 39 (1990): 260-61.

[25]Graves, *supra* note 21 at 5-6.

[26]Timothy George, "Is the God of Muhammad the Father of Jesus?" *Christianity Today* 46, no. 2 (2002): 30.

[27]Lauren Artress, *Walking a Sacred Path: Rediscovering the Labyrinth as a Spiritual Tool* (New York: Riverhead Books, 1995), 3-4.

[28]Artress and her followers have founded Veriditas, "the voice of the Labyrinth movement," dedicated to promoting use of the symbol throughout the world. They train facilitators and sell books, clothing, and jewelry on their website, veriditas.com.

[29]Deatra Walsh, "Walking on a Spiritual Path: Labyrinth of Peace Opens in August," Brandon University, accessed on November 10, 2007, http://outreach.brandonu.ca/Outreach/labyrinth.html.

[30]Abu-Nimer et al., *supra* note 2 at 25.

[31]Ibid.

[32]Ibid., 16.

[33]Ibid.

[34]Ibid., 25-26.

[35]Ibid., 37-41.

[36]Northrop Frye, "The Journey as Metaphor," in *Myth and Metaphor: Selected Essays 1974-1988*, ed. Robert D. Denham (Charlottesville: University Press of Virginia, 1990), 212.

◇◇◇◇◇◇◇◇◇◇◇◇◇◇◇◇◇◇◇◇◇◇◇◇◇◇◇◇◇◇

Bibliography

Abu-Nimer, Mohammed. "The Miracles of Transformation: Are You a Believer?" In *Interfaith Dialogue and Peacebuilding*, edited by David R. Smock, 15-32. Washington, D.C.: United States Institute of Peace Press, 2002.

Abu-Nimer, Mohammed, Amal I. Khoury, and Emily Welty. *Unity in Diversity: Interfaith Dialogue in the Middle East*. Washington, D.C.: United States Institute of Peace Press, 2007.

Artress, Lauren. *Walking a Sacred Path: Rediscovering the Labyrinth as a Spiritual Tool*. New York: Riverhead Books, 1995.

Chesebro, James W., Dale A. Bertelsen, and Thomas F. Gencarelli. "Archetypal Criticism." *Communication Education* 39 (1990): 257-74.

Frye, Northrop. "The Journey as Metaphor." In *Myth and Metaphor: Selected Essays 1974-1988*, edited by Robert D. Denham. Charlottesville, VA: University Press of Virginia, 1990.

George, Timothy. "Is the God of Muhammad the Father of Jesus?" *Christianity Today* 46, no. 2 (2002): 28-35.

Graves, Michael P. "Stephen Crisp's *Short History* as Spiritual Journey." *Quaker Religious Thought* 26 (1993): 5-23.

Labyrinths: Their Mystery and Magic. Directed by Richard Feather Anderson, Jeff Saward, and Robert Ferre. Russellville, CA: VisionQuest Video, 2000.

Langer, Susanne K. *Philosophy in a New Key*. Cambridge, MA: Harvard University Press, 1942.

———. *Feeling and Form*. New York: Charles Scribner's Sons, 1953.

Walsh, Deatra. "Walking on a Spiritual Path: Labyrinth of Peace Opens in August." Brandon University. Accessed 10 November 2007. http://outreach.brandonu.ca/Outreach/labyrinth.html.

Chapter 5

DELIBERATIVE DEMOCRACY AND INTERFAITH DIALOGUE: AN APPLIED PERSPECTIVE

Paul Fortunato and Diana I. Bowen

"The West must start a dialogue not only with 'the other' but also with itself."[1]

—Tariq Ramadan, *What I Believe*

Within the context of the university, public forums provide spaces for reflection, discourse, and deliberation. When we began the interreligious dialogue project at University of Houston-Downtown, our driving concerns were the pressing events in the Middle East and a desire to get beyond the knee-jerk reactions dominating the U.S. media in a post-9/11 world. Media of almost all political stripes have, at times on purpose, at times inadvertently, fed this reaction by so often linking the mention of Islam with images of violence and fanaticism.

Many people frame these discussions as a conflict between the West and Islam, following some version of the "Clash of Civilizations" model, which became a popular way of thinking after Samuel Huntington's book of that title. According to this model, the people of the West tend to have a worldview that is inherently and inevitably in conflict with people of non-Western, especially Muslim, cultures.[2] But we would argue that it is important to critique that framework, to point out the weaknesses in creating such a binary. In order to suggest alternative frameworks and messages, we have conducted interreligious dialogues on various topics. We hold the events under the auspices of the Center for Public Deliberation (CPD), part of our home institution, the University of Houston-Downtown (UHD). Founded in 2007 by communication studies faculty Drs. Windy Lawrence and Thomas Workman, the UHD Center for Public De-

liberation is "a non-profit, non-partisan, interdisciplinary organization engaged in educational and research activities surrounding public deliberation."[3] The primary mission of the center is "to encourage
the use of public deliberation by citizens as a means for civic choice-
making and problem-solving."[4] The vision at UHD is to see students
and Houston citizens actively and competently involved in deliberative democracy.[5] The Interreligious Dialogue project grows out of
the center's mission and holds an on-going series of public dialogues
across the three Abrahamic faith traditions: Judaism, Christianity,
and Islam.

The reasons for focusing on these three are the following. Many
areas of conflict in the world involve these three faiths. The program
planners desired to start with a limited number of faiths to keep events
from getting unmanageable. If we were to include all faiths, or even
major faith traditions, discussions could quickly become unwieldy.
Finally, we do not have any easy way of deciding where to draw the
line of whom to include. Any list of religions excludes many, and in
fact we would even have to work through the vexed question of what
constitutes a "religion," a concept that has a specific history, and one
that grew up in the West, mostly in relation to Christianity.

At the heart of this discussion is the concept of the public sphere,
a sphere from which religious revelation and discourse have tradition-
ally been excluded. As David Zaret points out, in the seventeeth and
eighteenth centuries when countries like England were developing a
secular public sphere, there developed a concept of "natural religion,"
a concept not tied to any one tradition. Zaret writes, "This appeal to
public reason in natural religion had immediate consequences for the
formation of a public sphere in politics. Banishing revelation from
religion made divinity irrelevant to political discourse."[6] However,
when societies refused the entrance of religious discourse, they un-
wittingly prevented much otherwise acceptable discourse from gaining access. The center's staff strives to make a distinction between religious discourse that is too partisan to be useful in the public sphere
and religious discourse that is sufficiently broad. Through the center's
interfaith events, we try to develop ways of defining such public, religious discourse and of setting up ground rules for making use of it.

Due to the nature of each individual topic and the composition pattern of invited speakers—community members, university professors, and students—the format of each public event required significant scrutiny. For example, the "God and the Commons" events planned and held in April and again in October of 2011 were run by faculty and student moderators and designed to be a series of discussions. These events included members of the community and were intended to be informative. Thus, a question/answer session is perhaps the most relevant part of this type of program. At first, the question/answer session used note cards, which would be collected and reviewed by members of the center before reaching the moderator. Screening preserved the anonymity of students or community members and encouraged people to ask honest questions. However, upon discussions, we decided to change the format for the next question/answer event. Students would have the opportunity to write their questions on note cards, as was the case in previous events, and they would also have access to microphones in case they wanted to ask questions directly. We found that this format helped us reach our goal for each of these events.

The Goal Is to Increase Trust

At the outset of our discussions, we typically encountered an emotionally charged atmosphere, in which many people, typically those within the Western traditions, react emotionally against what they understand Islam to be. The outset of our discussions, therefore, is typically imbued with emotion and not based on reason. At each of the center's events Muslim attendees have been put immediately in a defensive position. In the background of these religious discussions are other non-religious issues, for instance, immigration and the fear of lost jobs. As we said, our initial impulse was to help western Muslims, to give them a chance to set the record straight, or at least to clarify their situation. The events in which we explicitly included representatives of Islam in the discussion are summarized in the accompanying chart.

DATE	PROGRAM TITLE	FORMAT	PURPOSE
March 22, 2011	Ethics Conference. Interreligious Panel	Three student speakers, 25 minutes. Questions and answers, 45 minutes.	To have the students present the papers they had written on various aspects of interreligious dialogue.
March 8, 2011	"Judaism, Christianity, and Islam in Interreligious Dialogue: Abrahamic Faiths"	Three speakers, one Jewish, one Christian, and one Muslim, 30 minutes. Questions and answers, 45 minutes.	To have each speaker give a brief overview of his/her religion and then participate in a question and answer session with the student audience.
September 21, 2010	"The Muslim Community Center near Ground Zero"	Three speakers, one Christian, one Muslim, one unidentified, 30 minutes. Questions and answers, 45 minutes.	To discuss the rhetorical and ethical implications of the response to the proposed Muslim community center.
April 13, 2010 and October 12, 2010	"God and the Commons: The Place of Religion in the Public Sphere"	We used a published text called "God and the Commons," provided by the National Issues Forum, though we supplemented it in order to explicitly include Islam.	To have the students discuss religion and the public sphere, making use of a well-designed set of texts and discussion strategies.
February 25, 2010	"Islam, Judaism, and Hinduism: An Interreligious Dialogue"	One speaker from each faith, 10-minute introductions. Questions and answers, 45 minutes.	To have each speaker give a brief overview of his/her religion and then participate in a question and answer session with the student audience.
November 19, 2009	"A Visit to a Mosque: The Islamic D'Awah Center"	Twenty-five students and faculty toured a local mosque and observed a prayer service.	To give interested non-Muslim students a chance to tour the neighboring mosque in order to increase their knowledge of Islam.
November 5, 2009	"Islam and Christianity: A Student Discussion"	Thirty-five students sitting in a circle. Two students, both Christians, received training in order to organize this event, 90 minutes.	As with the April 13, 2010 event, the student participants discussed approaches to expressing religious ideas in public settings.
November 4, 2009	"Islam and Christianity in Interreligious Dialogue"	Two speakers from each faith (including two Muslim clerics and one Catholic priest) spoke for a total of 15 minutes. Questions and answers, 45 minutes.	To have each speaker give a brief overview of his/her religion and then participate in a question and answer session with the student audience.
April 6, 2009	"Islam and Christianity in Interreligious Dialogue"	One speaker from each faith spoke for 7 minutes each. Questions and answers, 45 minutes. We had no specific theme beyond dialogue.	To have each speaker give a brief overview of his/her religion and then participate in a question and answer session with the student audience.

In our initial public events, we placed substantive focus on Christians and Muslims in dialogue, and we left out Judaism. This was because we felt the most pressing need was to allow Muslims to speak publicly, as well as because we had severe time constraints and so ended up keeping the event as simple as possible. There are, of course, important benefits to including Judaism in the discussion. Not the least among these benefits is the need to address the Israel-Palestine conflict, something that has an enormous emotional impact on dialogues among members of the Abrahamic faiths. But we had to address this conflict without it becoming the sole focus of the dialogue event.

The center hosted a Hindu discussion as well, but the Hindu worldview appears to present a less pressing controversy given our time and place. Hindu Americans are not feared or distrusted in the same way that many Muslims and Jews believe they are feared or distrusted by the majority Christian faithful. If Hindus meet with apprehension, it is often because they are mistaken for Muslims.[7] Simply and directly, Islam was at the core of many national current events during the time the center was planning and hosting events: the Ground Zero Muslim Community Center in 2008; terrorist attacks by Umar Abdul-mutallab and by Dr. Nical Malik Hasan at Fort Hood in 2009; Tunisian and Egyptian revolutions in 2011 as well as ongoing uprisings that followed; and the Norwegian anti-immigrant, anti-Muslim terrorist attacks in 2011. They all made for pressing and substantive public deliberation.

◇◇◇◇◇◇◇◇◇◇◇◇◇◇◇◇◇◇◇◇◇◇◇◇◇◇◇◇

The Challenge of Religion in the Public Sphere: The Problem of Bringing Religious Discourse into Public Discussion

It is worth stepping back in order to consider some of the usual ideas related to the public sphere. Literature about the public sphere has a long history. One major thinker, Jurgen Habermas, conceptualized it as a space, separate from the state, in which people could come as equals and deliberate on issues of concern. These conversations of the public sphere, therefore, occur in a "private" realm of discourse that is used to hold the state accountable for its actions. This private realm of public discourse includes institutions like universities and schools, coffee shops and pubs, as well as various forms of mass media, the most powerful institutions of the public sphere. In other words, politicians and public officials operate in the public while the public sphere operates in the private realm where individuals discuss issues. Although world events provide opportunities for discussion, powerful media outlets often frame religious events and ideas in ways that perpetuate stereotypes. Thus, CPD provides an alternative space for students and others to engage in deliberative discussions, at times bringing religious ideas into play.

Habermas defines the public sphere in the following way:

> The bourgeois public sphere may be conceived above all as the sphere of private people come together as a public; they soon claimed the public sphere regulated from above against the public authorities themselves, to engage them in a debate over the general rules governing relations in the basically privatized but publicly relevant sphere of commodity exchange and social labor.[8]

In other words, citizens made use of the public sphere as a place where those concerned especially in commercial and social activity could operate, carrying out publicly relevant actions. But as Habermas writes more recently in his 2006 book co-written with Joseph Ratzinger, who became Pope Benedict XVI, the balance achieved by the modern public sphere "is now at risk."[9] This is "because the markets and the power of the bureaucracy are expelling social solidarity."[10] That is, modern societies tend to place highest authority on the market, as well as on the bureaucratic, supposedly-neutral procedural powers of the state. It is in response to this lack of "balance" that we are analyzing alternative models of the public sphere. Thus Habermas argues: "When secularized citizens act in their role as citizens of the state, they must not deny in principle that religious images of the world have the potential to express truth. Nor must they refuse their believing fellow citizens the right to make contributions in a religious language to public debates."[11]

As noted earlier, the center's staff makes a distinction between religious discourse that is too partisan to be useful in the public sphere and religious discourse that is sufficiently broad to be so used, depending on the context. It is a fact that in some contexts, speakers introduce religious discourse into public discussions without causing problems for people with different faiths or beliefs. In other contexts, however, religious discourse provokes considerable antagonism when it is introduced into public discussions. There are several problems that occurred in our public events and taught us some important lessons.

For example, at the center's Ethics Conference on March 22, 2011, one student presenter, Blithe Colgate, noted that we often exclude some main voices from public discussion because they are using religious discourse. She argued that this was weakening our public discussion when, for example, we face natural disasters or incredible loss of life. In the context of the Ethics Conference, Colgate discussed the disasters of Hurricane Katrina (2005) and the BP oil spill (2010). Her argument was that, when it comes to such disasters, religion is on many people's minds. In the case of the Gulf Coast of the U.S., which suffered doubly of these disasters, the dominant religious discourses are those of Protestant and Catholic Christianity. Even though not all Gulf residents are religious, many people regularly move into religious language. For example, with regard to both disasters, many people talked publicly about things like the dangers of not being proper "stewards of God's creation."

In another example, Colgate noted President Barack Obama's use of quotations from the Book of Psalms during his eulogy at the Tucson Memorial Service that followed the fatal shootings of six constituents of U.S. Representative Gabrielle Giffords in January 2011. President Barack Obama quoted the Bible. He remarked, partly in reference to the American people, partly in reference to Giffords, "As Scripture tells us: 'There is a river whose streams make glad the city of God, the holy place where the Most High dwells. God is within her, she will not fall; God will help her at break of day.'"[12] Colgate's simple, yet profound, point is that as people respond both rationally and emotionally to such disasters, it becomes difficult to refrain in public discussion from using some religious ideas and language.

We are thus reminded of the difficulty in finding the appropriate balance between religious discourse that is too partisan to be useful in the public sphere and religious discourse that is sufficiently broad to be so used.

The Challenge of Pluralistic Society: The Problem of Discussing Multiple Religious Perspectives

The large question then becomes how to use such religious discourse without being unfair either to people of other faiths or to non-religious people, how to ensure that religious discourse is sufficiently broad for public use. Again, the interfaith panel of the Ethics Conference, mentioned previously, provides a helpful case in point. One audience member registered some extreme discomfort with the idea of reintroducing religious discourse into the public sphere. He voiced the fairly common conception that the U.S. has definitively solved this problem by simply excluding religious discourse, thereby creating a purely rational discourse in the public sphere, and that the further solution to ongoing conflicts was to better police religious discourse. This audience member argued we should forcefully exclude anyone who would attempt to bring in such discourse and work better to educate young people that such attempts are forbidden.

One of the center's other events, "God and the Commons," addressed this concern as well. This event was organized by students with the help of faculty moderators in order to educate them on the importance of public discourse and deliberation.

The April 13, 2010, "God and the Commons: Does Religion Matter?" event made use of a text and a format created by the National Issues Forums (NIF) of the Kettering Foundation.[13] The format of the NIF text assures that it is not the speakers who do the discussing but rather the "audience." That is, the only people discussing strategies and solutions to the issue at hand are the people who attend the event. The organizers serve primarily an administrative purpose, providing the place and setup, though the moderators do participate with their ideas in a limited way also.

In preparation for the second "God and the Commons" event, which was held October 12, 2010, students in a senior level communication course studied the NIF text for several weeks.[14] The NIF text posits three possible approaches to the issue of religion in the public sphere. The senior undergraduates became familiar with the three options and were prepared to lead a public discussion about them.

The first approach is to "stay the secular course." Students explored the perspective that "religion belongs in the private sphere . . . but it shouldn't be a basis for public policy."[15] The second approach is to "recover our Judeo-Christian heritage." This perspective explains that "we should embrace religious values, especially those associated with our Judeo-Christian heritage."[16] The third approach is to "embrace religion's civic value" and essentially discusses the necessity for a neutral society where all religions have an equal voice. This perspective states, "We must not allow government to enforce one religious/cultural perspective on its citizens."[17]

On the day of the event, the audience gathered in a common room and was briefly introduced to the ground rules. The main rule for the event was that "this is a dialogue, not a debate." The group was separated into three subgroups, each accompanied by a student moderator from the course and a faculty moderator. After the groups had a discussion of each of the three perspectives in separate rooms, they rejoined each other, and the student moderators gave a short presentation about the key points in their small group discussions. One of the advantages of this format was that it increased audience participation. In small groups, people were able to voice their opinions without the fear of feeling conspicuous in front of a large audience. Students were also presented with more than two sides of an issue, which promoted discussion instead of debate. Finally, students examined each perspective and embodied it, whether they agreed with it or not. This promoted an examination of viewpoints before reaching decisions.

This October student-led "God and the Commons" discussion prompted thoughtful insights and commentary from attendees. Many student-participants voiced concerns that, if we were to increase the amount of religious discourse in public forums, our society would stand to lose some of the gains that have been made in increasing tolerance and acceptance of ethnic, religious, and other minorities. Such students voiced legitimate concerns. Other students responded that in spite of these concerns, it was desirable to work at including certain types of religious discourse. They argued, as do we, that religious people have to be willing to put themselves in uncomfortable discussions, engaging with unfamiliar discourses, when entering the public sphere in any Western society. One necessary element in public religious discourse is what some have called humility.

Another insightful idea emerged: non-religious people as well as religious people should also be willing to enter discussions in which their own discourses may be critiqued. All discussants need to understand that they do not have a monopoly on the universals, concepts like freedom, equality, justice, and progress. Each religion and worldview makes use of these concepts. We would generally agree with the Muslim theologian and philosopher, Tariq Ramadan, who writes of the importance of such "humility" in these discussions. We become humble, he says, "by admitting that nobody, no civilization or nation, holds a monopoly on universals and on the good, and that our political and social systems are not perfect."[18] Another point he makes is that "the West must start a dialogue not only with 'the other' but also with itself."[19] This is not, however, always easy to put into practice—there are several problems that arise when attempting to promote interreligious discussions in public forums.

The Challenge of Communication: The Problem of Preaching and Terminology from the Christian West

On November 4, 2009, the center hosted an event titled "Islam and Christianity in Interreligious Dialogue." For this Muslim-Christian dialogue event, most of the speakers were clerics, and at times they seemed unsure of how to address their audiences. These speakers were most accustomed to addressing their own co-religionists. Therefore, their dialogue tended to be a kind of hybrid between witnessing and discussing, between preaching and conversing. The speakers seemed to acknowledge that there is a lot of misinformation about religion perpetuated by the media. Part of their job as religious leaders, then, was to go back to the basics and discuss the basic tenets of their respective religions.

In the two Muslim-Christian dialogue events (April 2009 and November 2009), some of the speakers were, in fact, professional preachers and were not people used to or comfortable in the secular academic setting. The advantage of having such preachers as discussants was that they presented in an engaging, often charismatic, way and with an inspirational tone. The speakers presented their points of view and provided background on the history of their religion and its basic tenets. The disadvantage was that such a tone often makes interfaith dialogue a bit more awkward because the event takes on some aspects of a kind of competitive debate. Moreover, a perceived attack on one religion quickly becomes a personal ad hominem attack. Such are the levels of discourse that an event organizer must balance, and there is no perfect way to carry it out.

In the March 8, 2011, event, one audience member, who happened to be a Christian, asked both the Jewish and Muslim speakers, Rabbi Stuart Federow and Dr. Erkan Kurt, respectively, if they would be willing to let him bear a "testimony" to them. Federow frankly admitted that although in the past he had been willing to hear Christian testimonies of faith, he was no longer willing. He had heard dozens of Christian testimonies throughout his life, and he knew exactly what was going to be said. There was, therefore, no point in going through it again, the rabbi argued. It was interesting that the Christian man asking the question was in a "preaching mode" and did not have a detached, open conversational style. One of the points that Federow made was that if someone wanted to preach to another, that person would have to be willing to receive just as much preaching.

Rabbi Federow highlighted a unique challenge to public discourse during that event. He pointed out that most of the audience's questions, even those coming from non-religious persons, were framed in Christian terms. For example, one student asked how one pursued "salvation" through each presenter's religion. Federow responded that such a question did not entirely make sense to a Jew or a Muslim. The very term *salvation* has a specific Christian origin and has accrued many layers of meaning in the Christian West and more recently in the American South, the site of this series of public events. He stated that while Jews do approach God in order to seek union with him by means of his mercy, they did not necessarily see this in terms of a "saving" action. Nor do Muslims think in such "salvation" terms.

One fact that was not discussed at the event was that the very term *religion* comes out of the Christian West. Moreover, the specific northern European and North American history that informs American culture entails a certain conception of religion. What this means is that even atheists and agnostics in the West think about religion in very Christian ways. It is important to take stock of this heritage because often people are unaware of this fact. They tend to think that since they are not religious they stand in an equally open relationship to all religions.

When we were choosing speakers to invite, at first we gave little thought to it. The Christian speaker at two of the events was one of the authors, Paul Fortunato. When we eventually involved the Jewish community, we invited the already mentioned local rabbi, Stuart Federow, who created and hosts a popular interfaith radio program, "Show of Faith," on Houston KNTH Radio, 1070 AM. He was ideal for our purposes because he brought with him a broad listening audience and because he made interfaith dialogue a priority on his show. Since we could offer no honorarium, we found our first Muslim speakers by simply asking our university's Muslim Students Association to get whomever they could. This worked fairly well, and it ensured that the Muslim Students Association was comfortable with the speaker. However, program planners later found that it was helpful to work with the local Turkish community, which has its own Institute for Interfaith Dialog. Because they have experience with such dialogues, they proved to be ideal for our purposes.

Conclusion

With an understanding of the criticisms of Habermas' public sphere, we host events at the University of Houston-Downtown to generate dialogue that is inclusive of students and community members. We have experimented with formats for these events and have found through ongoing assessment that events may require a reexamination of the goals. If the event is informational in nature, for example, a longer question/answer session may be appropriate. If the event requires full participation from the audience, small groups help guide deliberation. In the end, however, each of these formats helps increase trust. Speakers may be put on the defensive and be forced from conversing into witnessing; however, there are many benefits of having these discussions.

This chapter examined the nature of public discourse as exemplified by the University of Houston-Downtown Center for Public Deliberation. After hosting several events, the authors explored themes that help explain issues with public discourse in the public sphere. Thus, public discussions are necessary to counteract less critical evaluations of public events and political decisions with critical thinking and dialogue. Our goal is to create a model for public discourse and to discuss those issues that make people feel uncomfortable within the university so that students and community members may be better prepared to discuss those issues at large.

∞∞∞∞∞∞∞∞∞∞∞∞∞∞∞∞∞∞∞∞∞∞∞∞∞∞∞

Notes

[1] Tariq Ramadan, *What I Believe* (New York: Oxford University Press, 2010), 6.

[2] Samuel Huntington, *The Clash of Civilizations and the Remaking of World Order* (New York, Touchstone, 1997).

[3] Windy Lawrence and Thomas Workman, *Proposal: The UHD Center for Public Deliberation* (Houston, TX: University of Houston-Downtown, 2007).

[4] Ibid.

[5] Ibid.

[6] David Zaret, "Religion, Science and Printing in the Public Spheres of England," in *Habermas and the Public Sphere*, ed. Craig Calhoun (Cambridge, MA: MIT Press, 1992), 225-26.

[7] Kate King, "Watching the Towers Fall, and Feeling his Turban Become a Target," *The Stamford Advocate* (Stamford, Connecticut). September 12, 2011.

[8] Jurgen Habermas, *The Structural Transformation of the Public Sphere*, trans. Thomas Burger (Cambridge, MA: MIT Press, 1991), 27.

[9]Jurgen Habermas and Joseph Ratzinger, *The Dialectics of Secularization: On Reason and Religion* (San Francisco: Ignatius Press, 2007), 45.

[10]Ibid.

[11]Ibid., 51-52.

[12]Barack Obama, quoted by ABC News. (January 12, 2011): http://abcnews.go.com/Politics/obama-speech-transcript-president-addresses-shooting-tragedy-tucson/story?id=12597444.

[13]The text we used is available at the NIF website: www.nifi.org.

[14]The upper-division students were all enrolled in the Communication Law and Ethics course. After discussing the three perspectives at length in class, the students were ready to be moderators and host a public event open to all students.

[15]Douglas F. Challenger, God and the Commons (Rindge, NH: New England Center for Civic Life, 2007), 1, http://www.nifi.org/stream_document.aspx?rID=10810&catID=15&itemID=10808&typeID=8.

[16]Ibid.

[17]Ibid.

[18]*Supra* note 1 at 22.

[19]Ibid., 6.

◇◇◇◇◇◇◇◇◇◇◇◇◇◇◇◇◇◇◇◇◇◇◇◇◇◇◇◇◇◇

Bibliography

Challenger, Douglas F. God and the Commons. Rindge, NH: New England Center for Civic Life, 2007. http://www.nifi.org/stream_document.aspx?rID =10810&catID=15&itemID=1080&typeID=8.

Habermas, Jurgen. *The Structural Transformation of the Public Sphere*. Translated by Thomas Burger. Cambridge, MA: MIT Press, 1991.

Habermas, Jurgen, and Joseph Ratzinger. *The Dialectics of Secularization: On Reason and Religion*. San Francisco: Ignatius Press, 2007.

Huntington, Samuel. *The Clash of Civilizations and the Remaking of World Order*. New York: Touchstone, 1997.

King, Kate. "Watching the Towers Fall, and Feeling his Turban Become a Target." *The Stamford Advocate* (CT), September 12, 2011.

Lawrence, Windy, and Thomas Workman. *Proposal: The UHD Center for Public Deliberation*. Houston, TX: University of Houston-Downtown, 2007.

Ramadan, Tariq. *What I Believe*. New York: Oxford University Press, 2010.

Zaret, David. "Religion, Science, and Printing in the Public Spheres of England."

In *Habermas and the Public Sphere*, edited by Craig Calhoun, 212-35. Cambridge, MA: MIT Press, 1992.

◇◇◇◇◇◇◇◇◇◇◇◇◇◇◇◇◇◇◇◇◇◇◇◇◇◇◇◇◇◇

Acknowledgments

We would like to thank the following faculty and students for participating in these events. We would also like to thank all who attended and listened to them including the following:

Derek de la Pena, Mike Duncan, Adam Ellwanger, Blithe Colgate, Helen Tsang, Michelle Wadsworth, Erkan Kurt, Rabbi Stuart Federow, Erik Luchetta, Alp Aslandogan, Chris Lane, Christina Rodriguez, Elise Rodriguez, Leah Scogin, Durim Tafilaj, Christina Guajardo, Ana Black Celis, Patricia Guerra, Imani Hughes, Natasha Marlow, Adriana Rodriguez, Mike Stastny, Ibe Uzoegwu, Doris Anderson, Ryan Davis, Brandon Feick, Jennifer Holloway, Joseph Tajik, Sean Ullrich, Matthew Wehmeier, Melody Witherspoon, Carla Bates, Jessica Castro, Kyle Ettinger, Danielle Johnson, John Kelley, Shaina Lucas, Brian Murray, Adriana Perez, and Tiera Williams.

Chapter 6

INTERFAITH DIALOGUE AND HIGHER EDUCATION: CHALLENGES AND OPPORTUNITIES

Jeffrey B. Kurtz and Mark R. Orten

"This is the great new problem of [hu]mankind. We have inherited a big house, a great 'world house' in which we have to live together—black and white, Easterners and Westerners, Gentiles and Jews, Catholics and Protestants, Muslim and Hindu, a family unduly separated in ideas, culture, and interests who, because we can never again live apart, must learn, somehow, in this one big world, to live with each other in peace."[1]

—Martin Luther King, Jr., *Nobel Lecture*

"The problem of the 21st century will be the faith line."[2]

—Eboo Patel, *Acts of Faith*

Calls for interfaith dialogue have taken on a new urgency. While the epigraph from King's Nobel Lecture does not explicitly name a principal reason for the urgency, we find ourselves in reluctant agreement with Douglas Jacobsen and Rhonda Hustedt Jacobsen, who remarked that "Much of the world's renewed awareness of and interest in religion is motivated by fear."[3] News reports and other media outlets confirm again and again in graphic flavors and colors the intense disputes between believers. The vitriol can seem overwhelming. And, of course, calls for interfaith dialogue are tied not only to fear, as scholars and theologians who recently met at the Templeton-Cambridge seminars on science and religion recognized.[4] Amidst these ruptures of fear and mistrust and hatred, woven in with pleas for greater understanding and civility, can we imagine conditions and commitments through which to promote examples of interfaith dialogue characterized by genuine authenticity? And how might such commitments and conditions be realized?

As Alexander Astin and his co-authors recently argued, higher education is a pivotal site for students' religious development, in that phrase's broadest sense. Observing that the "big questions" that occupy many students' lives (e.g., Who am I? What is my purpose in life?) are fundamentally spiritual questions, Astin and his collaborators maintain that "If students lack self-understanding—the capacity to see themselves clearly and honestly and to understand why they feel and act as they do—then how can we expect them to become responsible parents, professionals, and citizens?"[5] Colleges and universities provide unique forums where students may both practice and study the tenets of various religious traditions; through these practices and study, students become equipped to participate in American democracy with a greater sense of intentionality.

At the center of these practices and study, we believe, must be commitments to modeling and sustaining conditions by which genuine interfaith dialogue becomes more possible. Such dialogue, we hold is as, if not more, essential as any other dialogue across difference (e.g., racial, cultural, national, class, gender, etc.), for it goes to the heart of one's core commitments and ultimate values. It is identity with meaning. Moreover, to the extent that colleges and universities neglect this charge, we risk diminishing our democratic culture, an insight echoed in the recent work of Amanda Porterfield.[6]

Central to realizing such conditions for more authentic dialogue is re-imagining ways in which *rhetorical ruptures* might be recast as opportunities for critical reflection and faithful practice. We will elaborate on the concept of a *rhetorical rupture*; at this early stage in our discussion we wish to stipulate the term's similarity to what Thomas Farrell characterized as a rhetorical interruption, those symbolic examples through which is prompted the juxtaposition of "the assumptions, norms, and practices of a people so as to prompt a reappraisal of where they are culturally, what they are doing, and where they are going."[7]

This chapter seeks to present arguments around ways these *rhetorical ruptures* between religious believers may serve as foundations for opportunities for genuine interfaith dialogue. Such dialogue, we will show, is not tethered to familiar shibboleths about tolerance, getting along, or learning to live with difference.[8] Instead, the dialogue we envision is marked by conspicuously different features, ones concerned with, among other things, time, space, narrative, and seemingly irreconcilable practices and assumptions. Pivotal to the realization of these features, in part, is seeing with new eyes the kinds of positive yield that may be gleaned from rhetorical ruptures typically judged as harmful to efforts by interfaith believers to live together. Put another way, we need a deeper, more sophisticated understanding of the nature of conflicts between persons of different faith traditions and a corresponding recognition of how such conflicts may serve efforts to imagine and realize opportunities for interfaith dialogue characterized by authenticity and genuineness.

To help explain further the nature of the sort of dialogue we have in mind, we will undertake the examination of three case studies relevant to Denison University, located in Ohio, to uncover how these specific rhetorical ruptures may be understood as a kind of mosaic depicting ways interfaith believers might dwell together in a "world house." One such piece of this mosaic concerns a college president's efforts to steer his faculty toward conversations centered upon religion and values. The second case involves a campus community's efforts to promote dialogue across lines of racial and religious difference in the aftermath of incidents of public harassment and intimidation. The third mosaic piece will show in concrete colors the kinds of practices through which interfaith dialogue might be enacted and sustained on a college campus. These practices, as we will demonstrate, provide a vocabulary for discussion of religious differences, set an invitation for discussion of such differences, ensure safe spaces and protected times in which such dialogues may unfold, and offer practical actions of follow-through derived from the discussions that will aid a college's efforts to model what it means to talk across lines of faith-filled difference. The remainder of this chapter will, first, briefly survey assumptions around the rhetoric of religious pluralism, for this discourse, we believe, provides both opportunities and challenges to interfaith dialogue's realization. We then will proceed with a discussion of our three cases. Our chapter will conclude with insights we believe can be directly applied to local contexts where interfaith participants aspire to enact dialogues marked by authenticity and intentionality.

Rhetorical Ruptures and the Rhetoric of Religious Pluralism

Two primary terms serve as conceptual anchors for our chapter, and each requires brief explanation. First, we are committed to the close examination of what we have termed *rhetorical ruptures* on our campus and ascertaining the ways these ruptures may be productively re-read as suggesting insights and practices that might deepen our conceptual understanding of authentic interfaith dialogue. Stated succinctly, a rhetorical rupture may be understood as a pivotal moment when the conventions of rhetoric (argument, narrative, performance, in that term's broadest sense) inject conflict into a discourse community. Importantly, we do not view conflict solely as negative, nor do we ascribe to points of view that judge rhetoric in fashions cynical or shallow.

Such occasions of conflict may, in truth, present opportunities for education and understanding of the kind captured in the idea of what others have called *teachable moments*. Properly understood, then, rhetoric is a collaborative art concerned with addressing and guiding public judgment. Moreover, we echo the insight of Farrell who reminds us that our shared civic lives are "absorbed with projects, rituals of affiliation, and speech performances that ultimately turn on the mysteries of trust and fellow feeling."[9] These mysteries cannot be solved by the bureaucrat's chart or the spin doctor's manipulative tools. Instead, we must be ever mindful that rhetorical ruptures as we imagine them present us compelling choices clothed in ethical and aesthetic garb. Thus, in the cases we reflect upon in this chapter, each rupture is re-read to understand how it focused our campus's collective attention on potentially uncomfortable "truths" about religion, dialogue, and living together in community. We will tease out these cases to ascertain their ethical and aesthetic ramifications for interfaith cooperation.

This notion of interfaith cooperation brings us to the second key term central to this chapter: *pluralism*. At a most basic level, pluralism encompasses a commitment to "recognize and understand others across perceived or claimed lines of religious difference."[10] Given this commitment, pluralism would seem to commend itself across contexts and across spheres of encounter (religion, race, sexuality). The truth, however, is somewhat murkier, as scholars recently have articulated. Annalee Ward, for example, has raised objections to pluralism around questions of personal and professional identity. "To be faithful to one's own religious tradition, to be committed to its worldview as truth," she remarks, "sets one at odds to other religious traditions but also against those in the academy who scorn religion."[11] More broadly, Amanda Porterfield has critiqued the ways religious pluralism has been leveraged in certain professional historiographies about the evolution of democracy in the United States. At issue for Porterfield is when scholars laud pluralism as an ideal while simultaneously utilizing it as a framework for interpreting American religious history. Downplayed, she notes, are "alternative, less self-congratulatory scenarios of how national unity was achieved . . . and what role religion played in those activities."[12]

Along with embedded assumptions of unity as imagined in some historiographies of religion in the United States, pluralism also may be infused with presumptions of clearly defined differences between and among persons. In an essay concerned with ethics after pluralism, for example, Janet Jakobsen elaborates: such a model of pluralism "presumes clearly delineated 'units' of religious difference, most often located in well-recognized institutions of religious tradition with identifiable authorities."[13] The problems with such delineations are readily grasped: little or no recognition of diversity within these traditions, uncertainty over how to think through forms of religious difference that do not fit the neat contours such a model pluralism typically provides, inability to appreciate and understand institutions that fall outside recognizable (hierarchal) structures, and no grasp of how to talk about traditions where beliefs stand in second place to such things as practices or land.[14]

The breadth of opportunities and challenges associated with religious pluralism falls outside the scope of this chapter. We think it important, however, to offer a general cast of the idea, in no small part because any concentrated discussions about interfaith dialogue, and especially the ways we communicate difference between religious believers, must acknowledge the place of pluralism in such discussions. Its place, we recognize full-well, has been solidified within intellectual and religious landscapes because pluralism so thoroughly embodies the hallmarks and consequences of post modernity. What seems most pertinent to us, then, is the ways attention to pluralism, and its corollaries of difference and identity, cohere to create a continuum of perspective by which to think about and imagine what genuine interfaith dialogue might look like and the commitments required to sustain it.

Three points on that continuum are especially important. At one end, we have commitments to *exposure*. Stated succinctly, exposure may be understood as efforts by power-brokers within institutions merely to introduce religious difference into a given context. To amplify how exposure functions rhetorically and to render explicit its consequences for interfaith dialogue, our first case study will examine a brief proposal authored by a former president of Denison University in 1958 wherein he articulated how religion and values might be strengthened within the "instructional program" of the institution.

In the middle of the continuum may be found what we paradoxically term *disruptive marginalization*. We take this concept to embody commitments both personal and collective, tethered principally to notions of group identity and claims of injustice. More precisely, examples of disruptive marginalization are characterized by rhetorical ruptures articulated by putative outsiders, those regarded by occupants in the so-called "mainstream" as somehow different or exotic or "other." These ruptures specifically seek to marginalize institutions' taken-for-granted assumptions about their values and practices, thereby enabling the possibilities of beneficial, if oftentimes contentious and uncomfortable, critique. The importance of this place on the continuum cannot be overstated, even as it may be one that, more often than not, is caricatured by others as the bubbling over of mere frustrations or myopic political agendas couched in grievances of identity. In truth, disruptive marginalization invites us to reflect over our discourse practices and how these promote the realization of interfaith dialogue as we imagine it might be achieved. To further explain disruptive marginalization, we will consider a second case study, a series of incidents that divided our campus in the fall of 2007. Taken together, this collection of rhetorical ruptures presents opportunities to reflect over and articulate anew the essentials of authentic interfaith dialogue.

Finally, at the other end of the continuum from exposure, we find *authentic negotiation*. This negotiation is characterized by a set of rich principles and practices concerned with competing narratives, conflicting ideologies, irreconcilable practices, common ground, shared space, and the celebration of difference and unity. Our last case study will render in explicit fashion some of the ways the authentic display of these aforementioned principles and practices have been expressed at our university. We conclude with how they might be consistently realized as part of the efforts of colleges and universities to promote authentic interfaith dialogue on their respective campuses.

<hr>

Why an "Awareness of Values" Is Not Enough: The Problem of "Exposure"

In the fall of 1958 Denison University president Dr. A. Blair Knapp drafted a proposal that, by any standard of historical objectivity, might be rightly regarded as courageous and thoughtful. We advance this praise not because we necessarily share the foundational commitments on which that proposal was built, but because we admire the text's efforts to frame concisely and directly what President Knapp judged a vacuum in the intellectual life of the institution he led. As he remarked, while observers might assume that "value presuppositions underlie classroom teaching, the unfortunate fact is that, for the most part, the religious and value implications of any given subject matter are not openly faced."[15]

Knapp's spare "Proposal for Strengthening Religion and Values in the Instructional Program at Denison University" (it numbers just five and one-half pages) functions as a rhetorical rupture of import on two levels. First, as we will show through a careful reading of the text, the proposal attempted to give voice to what Knapp and others judged an alarming vacuum in Denison's curriculum: the absence of serious and thoughtful consideration of religious and moral questions as these may emerge across the academic program of instruction (and not just classes in Religious Studies, for instance).

The proposal, then, acts as a rupture concerned with matters of intervention. But there is a second, perhaps more significant, level we wish to explore. Namely, that while readers may judge Knapp's arguments with favor for their concision and focus on the potential for intellectual transformation, the text's principal act as a rhetorical rupture is to privilege an ethic of exposure. This ethic is characterized by narrow assumptions about religious, spiritual, and moral questions, and by an implicit faith in the value of sustained conversations with persons of allegedly greater experience, foresight, and wisdom, "a number of outstanding men in various fields whose careers have involved them intimately with vital religious issues and questions of value," as Knapp writes.[16] Bracketed in such a vision is the possibility for authentic interfaith dialogue, an authenticity characterized foremost not by expertise as much as by shared commitments to vulnerability and the collective desire to wrestle with these vulnerabilities across difficult questions centered on religious truths. An ethic of exposure, then, may function paradoxically to silence meaningful exchange over religious and moral questions.

As a rhetorical rupture characterized by an ethic of intervention, Knapp's proposal advances its case for a more serious, significant consideration of "religion and values" in three distinct keys. First, the cultural approbation for objectivity is turned on its head by muting that approbation within the context of a liberal arts college and recasting objectivity itself as something of a rash idea with its own value assumptions. As Knapp opens the argument,

> The liberal arts college with its traditional emphasis on the unification of knowledge and its concern for our cultural heritage should be an excellent place for transmitting religion and values. Unfortunately . . . the graduate schools, motivated by secular concerns, have encouraged scholarship of a

detached and specialized kind. The ideal of objectivity has been zealously cultivated [across scholarly disciplines].[17]

These arguments show their age, of course, but we are struck particularly by the emphasis given to context: a liberal arts environment should provide the opportunities for the meaningful transmission of religious values. But this context is not able to seize advantage because of the penchant for objectivity run amok. At work here, then, is an argument rooted in betrayal: because liberal arts colleges have given comfort to the "zealous objectivity" moving out from graduate programs, these institutions concerned with tradition, the unification of knowledge, and heritage are not fulfilling their social imperatives.

Along with recasting objectivity as its own faith, Knapp appeals to claims for open, full-throated inquiry that should characterize teaching and learning on college and university campuses. Science itself has long since left behind such archaic modernist notions of objectivity, while the larger enterprise of higher education seems still to cling to these with vexing irrationality. Questions of religious and moral values are not "openly faced" and an "unfortunate dichotomy" now characterizes much of what unfolds in the classroom with objectivity and a "life of reason" given pride of place in students' academic instruction, while "commitment and the life of the spirit" are relegated to the "extra-curricular" sphere.[18] What Knapp deftly executes over the breadth of the proposal is to underscore the common ground between scholarly, objective inquiry and considerations of religious and moral questions: that common ground is understood best as an openness to the questions which drive these respective spheres, questions that, if embraced across both spheres, could result in a restored "sensitivity" which ultimately may serve to infuse an instructor's teaching with a "new spirit and significance."[19]

Third and finally, Knapp's proposal carries through an ethic of intervention by underscoring for readers the gap between Denison's academic and "extra-curricular" programs, and specifically those programs concerned explicitly with religion. In the late 1950s, for example, Denison featured a weekly chapel service and an array of religious programs under the umbrella leadership of the Denison Christian Association. The existence of this gap, Knapp's explicit choice to highlight it in the way he does, provides him with an opportunity to argue for questions of relevance and impact and reach. That is, because the academic program has chosen not to engage in substantive fashion questions linked to moral and religious values, students' learning has been compromised. As he maintains, "It is our hope that with an opportunity to carry out the [proposed] program . . . we shall begin to bridge this gap and create an awareness of values with our instructional program comparable in its impact with that of the existing religious program."[20]

At last, though, the putative merits of Knapp's rhetorical rupture are deeply compromised within the second level on which the text works: one concerned foremost with what we term an ethic of exposure as the primary means through which to promote dialogue about religious and moral values.[21] Hopeful to "increase faculty awareness," Knapp and his colleagues desire to "initiate a series of faculty discussions in the area of religion and values." These discussions would be driven primarily by "a number of outstanding men in various fields whose careers have involved them intimately with vital religious issues and questions of value" and unfold over the course of a weeklong encounter, because "the communication of a person's religious outlook and sense of values would require fairly intimate association and that would be the optimum time for such association."[22]

As we remarked at the onset of this case study, Knapp's proposal has much to commend it, and we admire at some level the concern and thoughtfulness imagined in the potential of these respective weeklong encounters (six per academic year over a two-year period). And finally, we must still insist upon the weight of our primary thesis: President Knapp's proposal acts foremost as a rhetorical rupture driven by an ethic of exposure. The assumption beneath the proposed encounters seems to be that merely by putting Denison's faculty in the presence of "outstanding men," a greater "sensitivity" and concomitant significance to questions around religious and moral values will be realized. The problem with such an ethic for genuine, authentic dialogue is perhaps obvious: participants' agency is muted by the specter of exposure. The rhetoric of the seminar supersedes opportunities for the kinds of real vulnerability and risk that should be at the center of such encounters. Put a different way, the ethic of exposure hinders interfaith dialogue because its principal appeals are confined to recalibrating participants' intellectual assumptions. It is likely that attendees at the "intensive discussions" Knapp imagines would learn a good deal about the issues around religion and values raised by the guest speakers. We are not convinced, however, that the monolithic specter of exposure, with its commitments to a sort of passive acquiescence of intellectual assumptions about religious and moral values, is substantively sufficient to engender the transformation Knapp envisioned. Interestingly, the ethic of exposure in which he was immersed continues in different forms in our current age. We maintain an almost zealous faith that merely sitting around a seminar table together is sufficiently adequate to broach religious differences which may divide us. As the next case study will show, such a faith can be found wanting.

Listening at the Flagpole:
The Shortcomings of Disruptive Marginalization

Concerned with the nature of what we have termed disruptive marginality, this case study's relationship to interfaith dialogue between religious traditions may not seem apparent at first stripe. As is often the case, of course, it can be difficult to glean the insights and the wisdom amidst the rallies and the shouting and the fear that can disrupt a community, particularly when that fear seems to prey on hatreds tethered to race and sexual orientation.

But consider the following. In fall 2007 acts of vandalism and verbal abuse comprised of racial and sexual epithets marred the authors' home campus. Taken in isolation, any one of the single acts might have been readily explained, but their cumulative repetitive weight pressed down on the contours of community, resulting, as one writer reflected later, in amplifying the "sense of marginalization among a growing number of Denisonians who felt that they couldn't have the same peaceful and rewarding opportunities as others because of what made them different from the majority."[23] The tipping point happened thanks to a paper flyer advertising an a cappella group's annual

Halloween concert. That poster featured a hand-drawn noose and the invitation to "Come hang with the Hilltoppers." The group intended absolutely no harm, but the larger cultural context, not to mention the broader historical one, should have served as an object lesson, as the aftermaths of incidents in Jena, Louisiana, and Columbia and Maryland universities served as stark reminders of the inextricable relationship between the lynch mob's noose and racial hatred.[24] The incident with the a cappella group found its conclusion in fervent, sincere apologies and the sharing of viewpoints between the group and African-American students on campus. But the poster, to be sure, "represented larger issues," and it did indeed seem "time for the Denison community to pause, take hold, and speak its mind" about the "complacency, prejudice, and intolerance on campus." The poster, as our friend Paul Pegher observed with understatement, "started a conversation that couldn't—and shouldn't—be stopped."[25]

Those conversations—and rallies at the flagpole in the middle of the campus's academic quad, and sit-ins, and late-night conversations, and a campus-wide "time out" in November where nearly 2,000 participants gathered to address what came to be known as the "events of the fall 2007"—were by most measures quite remarkable and productive. The university's senior leadership made renewed commitments to see through initiatives concerned with promoting and sustaining diversity on campus; many students and faculty partook in rich conversations characterized by a refreshing civility and candor; the orientation programs for incoming students were recast in order to address directly the rich benefits of diversity to a college community; faculty proposed changes to the general education curriculum to encompass teaching about "some of the most difficult problems in American society"; and in January 2008 the State of Ohio awarded its first annual Dream in Action Award to the students, faculty, and staff of Denison, who collectively demonstrated commitments, as the citation read, "to direct positive action" and "promoting understanding, racial unity, and appreciation of diversity."[26] Finally, though, the events from that fated fall semester in 2007 leave us wondering about the staying power of what we have termed disruptive marginalization, particularly when that marginalization fails, in our judgment, to move a community toward deeper, more authentic understandings of the chords of unity and difference by which they are held together.

We want to be clear: the countless rhetorical ruptures that composed the fall of 2007 on our campus, the ways those ruptures cohered to focus our community's attention on pressing issues of racial and sexual and religious degradation, should stand as visible, pertinent reminders of how discourse tethered to disruptive marginalization may serve to heighten awareness of salient issues around justice, fairness, and the like. Gestures to authentic dialogue are not fully realized because the ethos of marginalization prohibits what we will demonstrate to be the more fulfilling habits of mind and corresponding discursive practices reflected in authentic negotiation. It is to a consideration of these habits and practices, reflected so richly provocatively in our final case, that we now turn.

∞∞∞∞∞∞∞∞∞∞∞∞∞∞∞∞∞∞∞∞∞

Creating the Space, Setting the Table, and Making the Invitation

If, as we have said, rhetorical ruptures in our community may constructively be conceived as occasions for mediation and negotiation among differences, then why not create a space in which this may happen, intentionally, for learning and growth? And so we have created *The Open House: Center for Religious and Spiritual Life at Denison*, which is "Dedicated to the Fine Art of Being Open."[27] In this former sorority house, rededicated in April 2010 to the ends of authentic interfaith dialogue and lived practice, we offer multifunctional rooms that have been renovated to accommodate a wide variety of religious and spiritual activities, including the following:

- Shoe-less Room for Prayer and Meditation
- Very Room for Roman Catholic Mass and Jewish High Holidays such as Yom Kippur and Passover, for Hatha Yoga and Interfaith Dialogue, for Quaker Friends Meeting and Ecumenical Christian Worship, and a multitude of other large group gatherings
- All Souls Kitchen for all things Vegetarian, including Shabbat Dinners for Hillel, Christian Bible Study, Iftar and Ramadan observanc-

es, and regular, ongoing Interfaith Dialogue

- Sacred Grounds Café for small gatherings of all kinds over Fairly Traded Teas and Coffees, for midweek Chai Tea with informal conversation and for rest and study
- Incubator for student leaders of religious groups and spiritual gatherings to discuss and plan and coordinate activities for themselves and with others
- Administrative offices for support and resources and the coordination of activities both at *The Open House* and across campus.

Our premier event at *The Open House* each week is a program that we call Denison Religious Understanding, where twenty or more students gather every Monday over a vegetarian dinner to discuss religion from their various places of familiarity. These include every week voices from such traditions as Hindu, Muslim, Buddhist, Zoroastrian, Jain, Sikh, Catholic and Protestant Christian, Mormon, Amish, and always, always a hearty, healthy dose of atheist and agnostic and searching constituencies. It is a very popular program that needs little explanation or enticement among undergraduates.

Our topics? Life after death: from the floating funeral pyre to the crematorium to birds picking the remains until gone to a pine box in the ground. Wedding rituals: from brides in red to brides in white to brides circled thrice under the chuppah, and the ritualistic significances of each. Truth (with a capital "T"), truth (lower case "t"), and truths (plural). It is here that we live out the charge of the Rev. Dr. Martin Luther King, Jr. to live together in a "world house." Our purpose in all of this is *religious understanding*. Can anyone doubt the significance and the need for this in our world today? Once *The Open House* came into use, we began to have fascinating occurrences of rhetorical ruptures which, in the abstract, were predictable and good. In reality, however, these occasions continually challenge all of us at the core of our identities where we feel things deeply and are transformed only very slowly, when at all.

Consider, for example, the night two years ago when Hillel (our Jewish student organization) was finishing its Friday Shabbat dinner that is held every week in *The Open House* at sundown with candles and prayers. Before the Jewish students finished their meal and discussion that evening, several Muslim student leaders arrived with catered food to set out for their traditional iftar meal, celebrating the end of the fast of Ramadan. In that moment of transition, Jews and Muslims needed the same space at the same time. The result was a beautiful picture of what can happen when conflicts of interest become intentional moments of negotiation for the learning of each and the education of all. After the awkward moment of realization that a scheduling overlap had occurred and each needed the space simultaneously, the Jewish students quickly wrapped up their discussion, cleared, and rearranged the tables they were using in the Very Room (larger meeting space), allowing the Muslim students to begin decorating elaborately for a festive celebration that stood in stark contrast to the solemn Jewish conversation happening in anticipation of Yom Kippur, the Jewish Day of Atonement. The students, all mixed at this point, quickly put up stringed lights and threw colored cloths over dining tables, and in the vegetarian kitchen (that they were allowed to share due to that common denominator, being meatless) Jewish student leaders ladled out Somali rice dishes to Muslim faculty, students, and their guests. It was a heavenly scene!

This single example may demonstrate the way in which rhetorical ruptures are occasions for mediation and negotiation in which:

1. Distinctive narratives emerge with clarity
2. Conflicting ideologies come into focus
3. Irreconcilable practices are defined
4. Mutual objectives may be discerned
5. Common ground may be established
6. Shared space and time may be negotiated
7. Difference and Unity (not uniformity!) may be celebrated.

Still in our time we may ask, "What does it mean actually to have to live in a 'world house'?" What does it mean to share? Not to share one another's deepest ideologies or common everyday practices, indeed we do not always do that, but rather to share on that higher plane a mutual regard for the manner in which the other of us seeks satisfaction for our deepest longings; not conclusions, but longings … our longings to know our places in the world, to know our origins and our destinations, to know our highest and best contributions to the shared world—whatever answers we each may give to those longings?

To live in a world house is to know ourselves and the truths by which we live and to seek to understand others' truths by which they live. To learn to share the wisdom that our truths have taught us and to listen truly to the truths of others. For some, these truths are carried by tradition, and for others they are written in the script of Nature or in the recitative of divine revelation breaking in on human history. Whatever its source, each has something to add to our knowledge and to our understanding—of ourselves, of our places in the world, of our work, and our happiness.

For far too long, we have lived religiously within a paradigm of scarcity, staking our claims on vast territories for nuggets of valuable Truth and failing to acknowledge the riches not only in our midst, but abundant riches within the beliefs and practices of others who may be different by consequence of history and geography—significantly different—but who are inhabited by similar quests and questions, similar essential needs and pleasures, similar aspirations and vocations. Now it is time for us to live into a different paradigm, a paradigm of plenty, of abundance, where each brings something for the good of all.

These are the challenges and opportunities of interfaith dialogue within higher education. We have not only the possibility for creating occasions of rhetorical rupture (this is going to happen whether we want it or not), we have the imperative! To this we have dedicated *The Open House* and all our education. On our campus a crucible for such learning has been created that resembles a great experiment in the nation and abroad with regard to religious difference. This religious difference is not exclusive to the three major, monotheistic, Abrahamic traditions (Christianity, Islam, and Judaism), but the same principles apply. Theological and other hierophantic differences need not be determinative in whether or how we live together harmoniously. Rather, it is within the domain of our mutual and shared concerns that we must learn to recognize the demands of the "world house" in which we live.

Coda: On the Possibilities of Authentic Interfaith Dialogue

Rhetorical ruptures as we have theorized here should be imagined in ways that allow for the authentic mediation and negotiation of differences. Such ruptures necessitate actions that are commensurate with the principles inherent in dialogue—a difficult and worthy discipline/habit/way of living. We especially are moved by gestures of experiential theology that seem, almost, to suggest a common heartbeat.

If the insights of Eboo Patel and Martin Luther King, Jr., served to launch the work of this chapter, reflections from the sacred texts of Judaism, Christianity, and Islam will be the means by which we close. This closure is ever only temporarily, for in committing to interfaith dialogue we acknowledge that our circles of conversation, experience, and reflection never can be completely closed.

- "The foreigner residing among you must be treated as your native-born. Love them as yourself, for you were foreigners in Egypt." (Leviticus 19:34)
- "Whatever you did for one of the least of these brothers and sisters of mine, you did for me." (Matthew 25:40)
- "Do good to…those in need, neighbours who are near, neighbours who are strangers, the companion by your side, the way-farer (ye meet)." (An Nisaa 4:36)

Perhaps it will someday be so.

Notes

[1]Martin Luther King, Jr., "The Quest for Peace and Justice" (Presentation, 1964 Nobel Peace Prize Lecture, Oslo, Norway, December 11, 1964).

[2]Eboo Patel, *Acts of Faith: The Story of an American Muslim, the Struggle for the Soul of a Generation* (Boston: Beacon Press, 2007), xv.

[3]Douglas Jacobsen and Rhonda Hustedt Jacobsen, *The American University in a Postsecular Age* (New York: Oxford University Press, 2008), 11.

[4]Cathy Lynn Grossman, "After September 11th, Religion Can No Longer Be Ignored," *USA Today*, August 21, 2011, http://content.usatoday.com/communities/Religion/post/2011/08/911-religion-god-spirituality/1.

[5]Alexander W. Astin, Helen S. Astin, and Jennifer A. Lindholm, *Cultivating the Spirit: How College Can Enhance Students' Inner Lives* (San Francisco: Josey Bass, 2011), 2.

[6]Amanda Porterfield, "Religious Pluralism, the Study of Religion, and 'Postsecular' Culture," in *The American University in a Postsecular Age*, eds. Douglas Jacobsen and Rhonda Hustedt Jacobsen (New York: Oxford University Press, 2008), 188.

[7]Thomas B. Farrell, *Norms of Rhetorical Culture* (New Haven: Yale University Press, 1993), 258.

[8]Wendy Brown, *Regulating Aversion: Tolerance in the Age of Identity and Empire* (Princeton: Princeton University Press, 2006).

[9]Farrell, *supra* note 7 at 2.

[10]Courtney Bender and Pamela E. Klassen, eds., *After Pluralism: Reimagining Religious Engagement* (New York: Columbia University Press, 2010), 2.

[11]Annalee R. Ward, "Problems and Promise in Pluralism," *Journal of Communication and Religion* 27 (March 2004), 1-10.

[12]Porterfield, *supra* note 6 at 197.

[13]Janet R. Jakobsen, "Ethics After Pluralism," in *After Pluralism: Reimagining Religious Engagement*, eds. Courtney Bender and Pamela E. Klassen (New York: Columbia University Press, 2010), 32.

[14]Ibid.

[15]"Proposal for Strengthening Religion and Values in the Instructional Program at Denison University," submitted October 30, 1958 (author's copy), 1.

[16]Ibid., 3.

[17]Ibid., 1.

[18]Ibid., 1-2.

[19]Ibid., 2.

[20]Ibid., 3.

[21]Ibid.

[22]Ibid.

[23]Paul Pegher, "On Common Ground," Denison Magazine, Winter 2007-2008, 18.

[24]Ibid., 19.

[25]Ibid.

[26]Ibid., 18.

[27]"The Open House," Denison University, http://www.denison.edu/offices/religiouslife/the_open_house.html.

◇◇◇◇◇◇◇◇◇◇◇◇◇◇◇◇◇◇◇◇◇◇◇◇◇◇◇

Bibliography

Astin, Alexander W., Helen S. Astin, and Jennifer A. Lindholm. *Cultivating the Spirit: How College Can Enhance Students' Inner Lives*. San Francisco: Josey Bass, 2011.

Bender, Courtney, and Pamela E. Klassen, eds. *After Pluralism: Reimagining Religious Engagement*. New York: Columbia University Press, 2010.

Brown, Wendy. *Regulating Aversion: Tolerance in the Age of Identity and Empire*. Princeton: Princeton University Press, 2006.

Farrell, Thomas B. *Norms of Rhetorical Culture*. New Haven: Yale University Press, 1993.

Grossman, Cathy Lynn. "After September 11th, Religion Can No Longer Be Ignored." USA Today, August 21, 2011. http://content.usatoday.com/communities/Religion/post/2011/08/911-religion-god-spirituality/1

Jacobsen, Douglas, and Rhonda Hustedt Jacobsen. *The American University in a Postsecular Age*. New York: Oxford University Press, 2008.

Jakobsen, Janet R. "Ethics After Pluralism." In *After Pluralism: Reimagining Religious Engagement*, edited by Courtney Bender and Pamela E. Klassen, 31-58. New York: Columbia University Press, 2010.

King, Jr., Martin Luther. "The Quest for Peace and Justice." Presentation at the 1964 Nobel Peace Prize Lecture, Oslo, Norway, December 11, 1964.

"The Open House." Denison University http://www.denison.edu/offices/religiouslife/the_open_house.html.

Patel, Eboo. *Acts of Faith: The Story of an American Muslim, the Struggle for the Soul of a Generation*. Boston: Beacon Press, 2007.

Pegher, Paul. "On Common Ground." Denison Magazine. Winter 2007-2008.

Porterfield, Amanda. "Religious Pluralism, the Study of Religion, and 'Postsecular' Culture." In *The American University in a Postsecular Age*, edited by Douglas Jacobsen and Rhonda Hustedt Jacobsen, 187-202. New York: Oxford University Press, 2008.

"Proposal for Strengthening Religion and Values in the Instructional Program at Denison University." Submitted 30 October 1958. Author's copy.

Ward, Annalee R. "Problems and Promise in Pluralism." *Journal of Communication and Religion* 27 (March 2004): 1-10.

Chapter 7

A CASE FOR INTERFAITH DISCOURSE

Joel S. Ward and David Stern

◇◇◇◇◇◇◇◇◇◇◇◇◇◇◇◇◇◇◇◇◇◇◇◇◇◇◇◇◇◇◇

Introduction

Interfaith dialogue as a topic of scholarly research has more recently become an area of interest in the field of communication. Although interfaith dialogue has seen substantial discussion in journals and books of religion, international, and peace studies, it has only been in the last two decades that communication scholars have started to contribute to this conversation. There have, however, been substantial publications and research on the topic of dialogue by communication scholars since the early 1970s.[1] This work was first summarized by Richard Johannesen in his article, "The Emerging Concept of Communication as Dialogue," in which he identified "ecumenical dialogue" as one strain of dialogue studies that informs our contemporary perspectives on dialogue in communication scholarship.[2]

In this essay, we hope to further the contribution of communication scholars to the study of "ecumenical" or interfaith dialogue by looking specifically at two thinkers who have deeply influenced the study of dialogue in the field of communication: Martin Buber and Mikhail Bakhtin. The authors of this essay align themselves with these thinkers not only for their perspectives on dialogue but also because of their specific faith traditions. Martin Buber's thought was informed by his Jewish heritage. Likewise, Bakhtin's writing was influenced by his knowledge of and commitment to Christianity informed by the Russian Orthodox tradition. Just as these two thinkers were influenced by their faith, so also are the authors of this essay. It is from this perspective that we approach the notion of "interfaith dialogue" as a possibility for people of different faiths and religious traditions working together in a mutual commitment. Both Martin Buber and Mikhail Bakhtin provide a substantial theoretical foundation to the study of dialogue and for this essay a hermeneutic entrance into the learning achieved through our case study.

Of course, one cannot honestly approach the topic of interfaith dialogue from a purely theoretical perspective. Dialogue as an activity is fundamentally different at the level of interpersonal interaction. It is difficult to work creatively and productively when the two people do not share, on their face, similarities in belief and perspective. Our case study is one of faith positions as they conflict during the mutual work of curriculum development for a basic public speaking course.

Current trends in curriculum development focus on the integration of multiculturalism and diversity.[3] Although most welcome, this trend has introduced a greater level of complexity into curriculum development. In the present case, the level of complexity is further heightened by the structuring of the course around the university's core theme area of faith and reason. Not only did the course content need to address diverse student groups, but it also had to grapple with the variety of faith positions represented in any classroom. Courses in the core theme area of faith and reason were designed to have "students study how the interactions of religious faith and reason have been expressed and their relationship understood," and one of the primary learning objectives of courses in this theme area was for students to "articulate how religious faith can play a role in the critical analysis of social problems and in the choice of actions for their resolution."[4]

The question of how to integrate "reason" into a public speaking curriculum is not altogether uncommon, as the rhetorical tradition has long appealed to rationality and public consensus as foundational to the activity of public speech. However, the question of faith introduced a new facet to the curriculum because this required different definitional work. It was the creation of this course that made necessary a real dialogue between the authors about how they viewed their individual faith positions and how this translated into a more general definition that made sense for both course instructors and their students. Answering the question of how faith is defined required a considerable amount of effort because faith is often thought of as a private reality. This private reality needed a corporate expression in order to operate as an organizing theme in the course. Although the resolution achieved for the course did not require complete conciliation by either of the authors, it did involve recognition that the community of students and instructors was providing the exigency that prompted a solution. The individual faith positions of the authors were placed against the background of a larger faith community (a Catholic university), and faith as a course theme was translated historically as a tradition of commitment rather than a facet of personality.

This realization gave rise to the conditions for a dialogue as it is conceived by both Buber and Bakhtin. Buber's often cited notion of the "between" does help us understand the transition from disagreement to dialogue, but it is his metaphors of "mismeeting" and "encounter" that open up the authors' personal experience for exploration. Bakhtin's description of the conditions for dialogic interaction—those of faithfulness, undersigning, and relational subjectivity—reveal commitments that precede the more discursive moments of conversation, resulting in a creatively productive relationship.

The first two sections of this essay will introduce the thought of Buber and Bakhtin and their theoretical contribution as a hermeneutic lens for the case. In the third section of the essay, we will explain our case and, in general, discuss the progression of the course development, specifically the problems faced in integrating faith as an organizing theme. Following the case study, we will discuss how the thought of Buber and Bakhtin help us see, retroactively, the event of dialogue as it took place between the authors of this essay. Finally, we will highlight the metaphors of commitment, companionship, and community as they emerge from our discussion of the case.

Most importantly, the authors hope to show that interfaith dialogue can occur, but that it is not a goal nor an end in itself. Instead, interfaith dialogue is a moment that occurs when two people of different faiths encounter each other over a shared work. The dialogue occurs, not in the resolution of their work or even as an outcome of their shared activity, but instead as an event that is preceded by commitment. Interfaith dialogue is an event always preceded by a commitment to the activity of working together, to the effort of discursive conversation, to the grief of continued failure, and to the person present before one, willing to share in the task.

∞∞∞∞∞∞∞∞∞∞∞∞∞∞∞∞∞∞∞∞∞∞∞∞∞

Martin Buber: Between *Vergegnung* and *Begegnung*

The philosophical and theological richness of Martin Buber's work on dialogue offers an ideal starting point for our discussion of interfaith dialogue. It would be enough that Buber's metaphor of the "between" and his inventions of *Vergegnung* (mismeeting) and *Begegnung* (encounter or true meeting) provide an important hermeneutic entrance for interpreting this case study, but one of the authors also identifies as a Jew in the humanistic Jewish tradition that Buber helped to revive.[5] In this sense, Buber's approach can be said to both represent a means of understanding the interfaith encounter and provide the narrative ground for one of the participants.

Buber's concept of the "between" is essential in understanding his philosophy of communication. "The 'between' refers to the region of the relationship—a third entity that requires both self and other, but is more than the sum of them."[6] Buber's "between" is not a priori, but rather emergent in dialogue.[7] As opposed to the dyadic exchange of information, dialogue takes on a life of its own, and the "between" is the commonality of being in dialogue together. We do not use the expression "life of its own" lightly here. Life, its creation, and preservation are primary concerns in the Jewish tradition; it is no accident that life and dialogue are continually linked throughout the scholarship of and about Martin Buber.[8]

Additionally, dialogue and the "between" for Buber are not the same as the conversation in which the dialogic "between" emerges. The between emerges where two people walk "on the narrow ridge, where I and Thou meet, there is the realm of the 'between.'"[9] The metaphor of the narrow ridge illustrates the tenuous and perhaps threatening nature of dialogue. Interacting, we pass in and out of dialogue, from I-it to I-Thou, and back again. This is how we walk the narrow ridge and how the "between" emerges.

Stepping onto the narrow ridge appears to be dangerous enough;

stepping out with another person poses more danger still. "The 'between' is Buber's alternative to ideological camps, guiding Buber's existential message about dialogue."[10] One does not necessarily need to give up the narrative ground on which one stands, but to reach the "between" one must willingly leave behind the protective strictures of ideology. Dialogue requires openness to the possibility of change. Only when one willingly invites the other onto the narrow ridge can the "between" emerge, and the dialogue comes to life.

Although scholars in communication have elaborated on our understanding of Buber's metaphor of the "between," little attention has been paid to his concepts of *Vergegnung* and *Begegnung* beyond the story of their origin. Buber discusses his childhood without his mother in *Meetings*.[11] He tells the story of a conversation he had as a child with a little girl about his mother, to which the girl responds, "No, she will never come back." Friedman explains that as a young scholar Buber coined the term *Vergegnung* to describe the "mismeeting" among men (and women) in juxtaposition to *Begegnung*, a true meeting or encounter.[12] Some twenty years later, Buber was reunited with his mother in a brief visit, "I could not gaze into her still astonishingly beautiful eyes without hearing from somewhere the word '*Vergegnung*' as a word spoken to me."[13]

Psychology and psychoanalysis have utilized the ideas of *Vergegnung* and *Begegnung* much more than have dialogue studies. These concepts, particularly *Vergegnung*, are often understood in the context of the relationship between the therapist and the patient(s).[14] Fishbane explains that such mismeetings occur when the therapist fails to be empathetic to the patient: "These moments of 'mismeeting' are painful, but they provide potentially rich opportunities for the therapy. If the therapist can manage not to be defensive about these moments, can be open to the couple's responses, and can take responsibility for his or her part in the mismeeting, then these moments can be rich and productive. A moment of mismeeting can then be transformed into a moment of healing."[15] Although the notion of empathy is clearly not a part of Buber's dialogue, it is debatable as to whether or not he would consider mismeetings, in the sense of *Vergegnung*, to be such golden opportunities.

The term *Vergegnung* implies not simply a mismeeting in the present that may be salvaged; *Vergegnung* is also a missed-meeting that has passed. When we invite the other into dialogue, we step onto the narrow ridge. We are not only vulnerable to the insincerity or manipulations of the other, we also risk a mismeeting, a missed opportunity to be in dialogue. *Vergegnung* is a concept inherently laced with regret; even when *she* comes for a visit we remember, "No, *she* will never come back."

Conversely, *Begegnung* is when we meet the other as other. We do not pass by one another with pleasantries or jargon, but instead we enter into a relationship in which we are cognizant of the distance between us. Wolfson explains that "Buber himself has told us, the entering into relation, and, we might add, the sustaining of that relation, presupposes the setting at a distance."[16] *Begegnung* may be the moment it becomes possible for us to step onto the narrow ridge. Meeting in the distance of otherness that makes you so other from me is, for Buber, how the "between" may emerge as a third party and as common ground.

Mikhail Bakhtin: Faithfulness to Dialogue

An honest study of dialogue means acknowledging thinkers such as Martin Buber and Mikhail Bakhtin. In fact, it is argued by some scholars that Bakhtin follows both Buber's work and his specific terminology.[17] Contemporary dialogue scholars consider Bakhtin's work foundational to the study of dialogue,[18] and his ideas have extended the scope of dialogue beyond the study of language to being "implicated in the modern history of thinking about thinking."[19] This, of course, means that for Bakhtin dialogue is more than a theory about the means or the how of human communication. It is in a sense the underlying design of Bakhtin's philosophy of human action. This means that dialogue is an idea that moves substantially in all of his writing. For this reason, we will not attempt a full exposition of his thought on dialogue but will instead point to significant concepts important for our present case. We will lean heavily on the work of Michael Holquist and his book, *Dialogism: Bakhtin and His World*, in which he summarily covers Bakhtin's thoughts on dialogue and his idea of *dialogism.*

Holquist is first very clear that "dialogism itself is not a systematic philosophy."[20] Instead, it is a focus on the relationship between human beings and, more specifically, between active personalities. In one way, dialogism is a means of viewing human interactions as primarily subjective in nature, with a stress on the relational nature of that interaction. Because of the emphasis on subjectivity and relationship, Bakhtin considers the participants in any dialogue as highly reliant on one another and states that in any human interaction there is no "figure without [this] ground."[21] This is no self-established position but rather one that is given because one is never in complete control over both the situation and the circumstances in which one finds oneself. There is "giveness"[22] to the ground that I stand on to orient myself in the world and in my relationship to others.

This "giveness" is not, however, a simple determination of who I am or with whom I relate. With the ground I am given comes a responsibility to play an active role in relating. For dialogue to be possible, I must take ownership of the place in which I stand. For Bakhtin, this means that I must be willing to "undersign" my position,[23] take responsibility for where I stand, and most importantly preserve the uniqueness of my position. The maintenance of my position is an essential piece of dialogic interaction because the collapse of one's position into the positions of others who relate to me is an end to the dialogue.

It is important to note that Bakhtin's account of dialogic conversation is not often a prescriptive one. Instead, he is intent on describing the elements of dialogic speech between two or more people. Bakhtin is convinced that although monologic forms of speech are attempted, they are a ruse, never fully acknowledging nor responding to the voices at play both internally and externally in every speech event. On the contrary, Bakhtin notes that "Because of its simplicity and clarity, dialogue is a classic form of speech communication. Each rejoinder, regardless of how brief and abrupt, has a specific quality of completion that expresses a particular position of the speaker, to which one may respond or may assume, with respect to it, a responsive position."[24]

Truly dialogic speech then is a disclosure of one's position so that others can take a position in response to it. As stated earlier, a speaker must be willing to undersign her position and disclose its parameters in order that others who converse with her may be able to truly respond to her stated position. If I were to evade the responsibility of undersigning my position, I would make it at the very least difficult and at most impossible for the person I am speaking with to respond in kind. By undersigning my position, I make clear internal and external boundaries that show the individual and unique nature of my position. The boundaries demarcated by speaking from one's own position enable the responsive position of those with whom one speaks. We include here an extended quote that we think clearly demonstrates how Bakhtin envisions the activity of dialogic speech as both an individuating and unifying event. In his discussion of genres in his later essay, "The Problem of Speech Genres," Bakhtin writes:

> They, too, are clearly demarcated by a change of speaking subjects, and these boundaries, while retaining their *external* clarity, acquire here a special internal aspect because the speaking subject—in this case, the *author* of the work—manifests his own individuality in his style, his world view, and in all aspects of the design of his work. This imprint of individuality marking the work also creates special internal boundaries that distinguish this work from other works connected with it in the overall processes of speech communication in that particular cultural sphere: from the works of predecessors on whom the author relies, from other works of the same school, from the works of opposing schools with which the author is contending, and so on.[25]

Bakhtin's description outlines what he sees happening in the development of specific speech genres or areas of different cultural activity. In this description, he is clear that the author of a new work—or, in our case, a person in conversation—creates something unique because of her place in time and her particular point of view. This point of view is not, however, set apart in the world of ideas or independent from a historical legacy. In fact, the speaker, as she speaks, simultaneously shows her unique personage while also connecting herself to the history informing her perspective, as well as to those who might hear and respond to her words; "a rejoinder in dialogue."

It is tempting to see the relationship between the unique voice of the speaker and the relational and historical nature of her position as dialectical, but for Bakhtin dialogue moves beyond this dualistic tension. As Holquist notes, "dialogue is not a dyadic, much less binary, phenomenon."[26] Besides the positions of the two people in conversation, there is a third element to dialogic relations that is always present in a dialogic event. Similar to Buber who identifies a "between" in dialogue, Bakhtin describes how the a priori relationship between two people in conversation shapes what meaning will come of the speech acts. Alan Jacobs suggests that Bakhtin characterizes this a priori relationship as a loving relationship, one that sets the conditions for a dialogic conversation.[27] Holquist describes this "thirdness" in Bakhtin's view of dialogue as bearing "the seeds of hope"[28] because it creates the potential for any meaning that a speaker attempts to convey to find a relationship that will both understand and respond to that attempt toward meaning.

Both hope and love as elements of the relationship that enables dialogue are reminiscent of the openness and subjectivity in Bakhtin's descriptions of dialogic speech acts. It is from this position that Bakhtin addresses the problem of unique individuality alongside common understanding or shared perspective, the hopeful or anticipated outcome of a dialogic interaction. One would think that for individuals to come to consensus they have to concede their unique position for one that is shared with others. This is not so for Bakhtin. This loving hopefulness is not a position of passivity, nor an openness that demands one relinquish one's position. Instead, Bakhtin describes unity as possible only through *faithfulness*[29] to one's position *in the relationship*. This is not a "contextual constancy of a principle, or a right of law"[30] but instead constancy like that expected in "marital love."[31]

We cannot, with the space given, do justice to the depth of this idea, but this invoking of a marital relationship demonstrates that Bakhtin's notion of dialogue focuses our attention toward the prior relationship and unique interpersonal disposition that precedes the conversation of two people. A faithful commitment to a relationship and an acknowledgement of its fragile immediacy situated within a larger sphere of discourse both preserves important boundaries and allows the necessary openness for a dialogic interaction to be sustained.

To conclude this theoretical exploration into the character of dialogue as understood by the authors, we want to summarize what both Buber and Bakhtin reveal for the following case. The concept of the "between" as an emergent third element of dialogue is foundational to examining nearly any encounter through the lens of Martin Buber. In addition, we will use the ideas of *Vergegnung* to discuss the pattern of mismeeting or missed opportunities for dialogue.

For Bakhtin, all dialogic interaction is relational, dependent on those with whom we speak. Foremost, it requires that I undersign my position, being willing to stand on the ground I am given in order to provide others with a point of orientation and an opportunity to respond. This undersigning is an a priori commitment to the others with whom I speak and a faithfulness to relationship as both the ground and the position for which I am answerable. It is from this lens that we explore the following case.

The Case: Collaborative Development of a Public Speaking Course Curriculum

Extending far beyond the study of interpersonal communication into a larger field of scholars and practitioners, the verbiage of dialogue is often employed to invoke a genre of communication that is more egalitarian, inclusive, and communal, rather than individuating or sectarian. The assumption that dialogic forms of speech are more likely to bring individuals and groups together is the basis of most contemporary public speaking pedagogy, which in some cases specifically references the "dialogic perspective."[32] Dialogical communication can, however, often be more revealing of differences between those in conversation. If the persons in conversation come from very different philosophical and theological positions, it follows that what emerges from the encounter will more likely be boundaries between their positions rather than a platform of common understanding. It is exactly this kind of scenario that serves as the impetus for this essay and the subject of our case.

The case we explore in this essay is the development of a public speaking curriculum, informed by the categories of faith and reason. The development of the course was a cooperative project including both faculty and graduate student assistants, although a significant portion of the creative work and effort was turned over to the graduate students once the course shell had achieved approval from advising faculty and a university core curriculum committee. The categories of faith and reason framed the course because it was designed to fit into a larger core theme area designated by the university as a significant and important area of learning. It was thought that to speak publicly one must first be able to acknowledge one's own position and then provide reasonable arguments for maintaining and protecting that position in the public sphere. The acknowledgment of one's position was considered to be a position of faith because all ideological positions are somewhat dependent on presuppositions that cannot be absolutely proven.

It is for these reasons that the course was designed to encourage students to inquire after their own personal positions—political, ideological, or religious—in order to deepen their understanding of their dependence on unempirical presuppositions. Having achieved this, students were instructed to work on developing reasonable arguments for their position. They were also encouraged to acknowledge that their own presuppositions required a certain amount of individual faith in the validity of these foundational assumptions.

The introduction of faith and reason as organizing categories for the course proved to be a significant challenge not only for students of the course but also for those responsible for its construction and implementation. The two graduate students charged with the course as graduate student directors themselves struggled to find a common position regarding the relationship between faith and reason. Differences immediately arose when it came time to define faith as an organizing term for the course. The graduate student directors were of differing opinions because of their own faith positions, one religious and the other socio-cultural. To be more specific, one of the directors was committed to a Christian worldview, whereas the other self-identified as an atheist with a commitment to Jewish heritage, contemporary Jewish culture, and the global Jewish community.

The difference of position became glaringly evident in the directors' attempt to provide a general definition of faith for the course and formulate how this faith influenced the reasoning of a given public speaker. Initially, the directors approached the difference dialectically. The practicing Christian interpreted the stance of his colleague as "faithless" or without faith and, therefore, weak as a position from which to reason. The Jewish atheist found the Christian's position inflexible and in some ways privileging "people of faith" over and against himself and students that may or may not align with a more widely recognized religious perspective. This inflexibility he believed to be quite unreasonable both for course design and pedagogical practice. This was an initial difference that would manifest itself later as the course was introduced to students. Initial resistance to the theme of faith was presented by students who believed that the introduction of this guiding term made the topic of public speaking too closely associated with religious faith.

The preliminary difference between the course directors in course construction was initially resolved by the introduction of additional material which represented a third perspective—that of catholic intellectual thought. The book *Reason and Revelation in the Medieval Ages* by Etienne Gilson[33] developed multiple possibilities regarding the relationship between faith and reason, tracing their historical development during the medieval period. This material introduced students to differing philosophical perspectives regarding the interaction between faith and reason. This material was introduced to the students through a series of lectures framing the coordinates of faith and reason for the course. This difference in course design did not attempt to end the difference in perspective because it offered multiple perspectives regarding the relationship between faith and reason. Within this spectrum were perspectives that described faith and reason as oppositional, complementary, and sequentially prerequisite. The last of these perspectives was adopted as the primary perspective in the course. This perspective described reason as reliant on the faith position that preceded it, a position that found its origin in the work of Augustine of Hippo who is often credited with the idea that in order to understand (apply reason), one must first believe (have faith).

The adoption of this position regarding the relationship between faith and reason still posed some problems for the course directors. Although choosing one position for the course reconciled some of the debate over how to define "faith," it did not resolve the question of implementation. The question of how the directors of the course with differing perspectives would be able to consistently direct the graduate instructors on how to articulate this relationship was not easily answered. What began as a question of implementation quickly became the broader question at the root of every interfaith conversation.

The question that was quickly apparent to both directors was a question of epistemology. From the perspective of the director who was a practicing Christian, there were some things that could only be understood if one believed in them first. From the perspective of the director who was an atheist Jew, to state that something must first be believed before it could be understood was a claim to exclusive or revelatory information, a notion that was resistant to his understanding of reason. In essence, the practicing Christian could not fathom a position that did not first acknowledge a faith system, and the atheist Jew could not understand a faith that did not observably adhere to boundaries of a common reason.

This fundamental difference between the two directors emerged after numerous conversations about how to guide new instructors of the course in its implementation. These conversations grew in frequency as new instructors were faced with questions from students regarding the course coordinates of faith and reason. This produced a second question that needed an answer. How could two people who had faith in different things reason alike? This was a significant problem, not just for course implementation but also for the general basis of the course. Public speaking itself was proposed as a speech activity that could create consensus, bring together differing perspectives around one purpose, and create linkages between people of differing faith positions. If those charged with designing and implementing the course could not resolve this difference interpersonally, how could instructors be shown the way to explain and demonstrate this activity in the classroom? This is a question that would need some resolution if the course were to be successful and its leadership consistent.

Attempts at answering these questions were made during lengthy conversations as the directors sought to resolve their differences of position for the purpose of providing complementary answers to course instructors. It was this common task that eventually provided the ground for a change that would propel the conversation forward from disagreement to meaningful dialogue. The questions of the larger group of instructors refocused the discussion away from the dialectic of the two positions represented by the two directors and toward the instructors and students in the course itself. Previously, both directors had attempted to control the content of the course by privileging their own positions over the common work necessary for a reasonable agreement on the terms of faith and reason. This task had presented itself before the differences had demonstrated themselves in the course construction and in the initial stages of implementation. However, the conversation had neither recognized nor acknowledged the importance of the common task: a clearly articulated course design and pedagogy. The greater community of instructors and students for which the course was intended called for conciliation on the part of both directors in order that the necessary work—the instruction and performance of public speeches—could be achieved.

The outcome of this case showed that it was the commitment to a shared task and to continued companionship which preceded the development of a fruitful dialogue, producing the necessary conciliation for the work to be accomplished. Up until the acknowledgment of the community, this "interfaith" conversation was less dialogic and much more discursive. In fact, the coming together of individuals of differing faith positions, highlighted by the structure of the public speaking curriculum, was a moment of discursive difference rather than dialogic understanding. The authors of this essay conclude from this case that dialogue is not a prerequisite form of discourse but rather an event that can occur through commitment of two people with opposing positions toward each other and toward an already present community.

Commitment, Companionship, and Community

It is tempting to say that dialogue can and will happen when the proper circumstance is given or when a space emerges in discourse that allows for honest conversation. This is only somewhat true for the case as it is presented here. The introduction of a third voice was what called the authors out of themselves toward a new relationship, to work "between" themselves rather than within their own faith positions. Moreover, because this third voice took the form of different course instructors and students, little could be said about a particular faith position. The dialogic "third" that did emerge was, in fact, a pedagogical space between *people* of different faiths, not between their differing faiths.

It was not only a physical or communal space that prompted the dialogic interaction of interfaith proportion but rather a commitment to a companion for a given task. This is not to say that the authors' beliefs about the other's position did not change at all. What occurred was not the emergence of a third space that comfortably included two fundamentally different positions. Rather, a relationship of commitment and a growing companionship changed the way those positions were seen and understood. Not that the authors' positions had become more similar, but that they could find value in the other position through relationship with a unique person.

Martin Buber's concept of *Vergegnung* encourages us to see the initial "mismeetings" and disagreements of the course directors in constructive light. By entrenching themselves in their faith positions and not acknowledging the possibility of third voices, conversations about constructing the course became arduous, a wholly unpleasant task. A genuine sense of dislike for conversation regarding the course was present with every attempt at agreement. Even when progress appeared to be forthcoming, one or both directors might say something that would collapse any progress that had been made. Every meeting ended without tangible results, leaving the authors regretful of the wasted time and effort. Until the introduction of the third voice or voices, the project was indeed a *Vergegnung*, a "mismeeting."

Oddly enough, the authors began to share the grief of repeated failure and through this shared discouragement became aware that the other was equally committed to the success of the task. Mutual regard developed into an earnest companionship. The sense that "we are wasting our time" became more a feeling that "this conversation may be fruitless but we must keep trying." If a "between" did emerge, as Buber would have it, it emerged only out of mutual disdain for further failure and the hope of achieving some level of resolution.

Although the concept of *Vergegnung* illuminates the regret of missed opportunities in the relationship of the course directors, Buber's notion of the "between" as an emergent third party in a dialogue only demonstrates that this could not be interfaith dialogue. The more faith became a part of the conversation, the more adversarial the conversation and the relationship became. It was only when the directors heard the third voice, that of the community of instructors and students they were tasked to serve, that any progress was made toward the course's completion. They became accountable to each other to move beyond the wrangling of opposing faith positions toward a solution that would serve the community. This accountability to each other was the seed of a creatively productive companionship.

The notion of companionship is where Bakhtin's understanding of dialogue helps us see further into the dependent nature of speech in the context of human relationships. The authors' recognition of a developing companionship, acknowledged and supported by the voices of other colleagues, created a shared position with which to view the work of creating the course. It was "faithfulness" to differing positions and the resulting failure of agreement that produced a relationship of filial character.

By "undersigning" their positions, the authors provided points of orientation, coordinates for each other to understand the boundaries that stood between them. Clearly seeing these boundaries, the depth and breadth of them, gave both authors an appreciation for the positions themselves, as well as for the person who held them. It was, in a sense, the *subjective* boundaries that became the common ground for the work to be accomplished. Because the boundaries maintained the ideological, intellectual, and theological differences between the two authors, they became more reliant on the relationship that sustained their work rather than hope in the possibility of a shared position. As coauthors and former course co-directors, we still disagree about definitions of faith and the positions of faith that we both firmly hold. There is no unity of an ideological or theological nature. There is only unity in the "answerable" nature of our positions toward each other. We are as companions in work, accountable *for* each other and *to* each other. It is not, however, the work of the creating of any given course but the work of the encounter that prompted a dialogue. The effort, the willingness to continue struggling, is what led to an achievement, if only a momentary one. The resolution of our disagreement was not on some common ground about what faith is for a public speaking curriculum but through continuing to be answerable to each other as friends and scholars. The realization and recognition that even these conversations had implications in the community were voices that called to and were heard by both of us. This essay serves as a representation of that momentary achievement, reminding us that it is only the *project* of interfaith discourse that achieves interfaith dialogue and that dialogue itself is an event in human conversation that cannot be easily discovered or sustained.

Notes

[1] Ron C. Arnett, Celeste Grayson, and Christy McDowell, "Dialogue as an Enlarged Communicative Mentality: Review Assessment and Ongoing Difference," *Communication Research Trends* 27, no. 3 (2008): 8.

[2] Richard Johannesen, "The Emerging Concept of Communication as Dialogue," *Quarterly Journal of Speech* 57, no. 4 (1971): 373.

[3] Lori J. Carrell, "Diversity in the Communication Curriculum: Impact on Student Empathy," *Communication Education* 46, no. 1 (1997): 234-44.

[4] "Founding Document," University Core Theme Area, 2008-09.

[5] Laurence J. Silberstein, "Martin Buber: The Social Paradigm in Modern Jewish Thought," *Journal of the American Academy of Religion* 49, no. 2 (1981): 211-29.

[6] Kenneth N. Cissna and Rob Anderson. "Communication and the Ground of Dialogue," *The Reach of Dialogue: Confirmation, Voice, and Community*, eds. Rob Anderson, Kenneth N. Cissna, and Ronald C. Arnett (Cresskill, NJ: Hampton Press, 1994), 23.

[7]Lisbeth Lipari, "Listening for the Other: Ethical Implications of the Buber-Levinas Encounter." *Communication Theory* 14, no. 2 (2004): 130.

[8]Martin Buber, *The Letters of Martin Buber: A Life of Dialogue* (Syracuse, NY: Syracuse University Press, 1996). Maurice Friedman, *Martin Buber: The Life of Dialogue* (New York: Routledge, 2002).

[9]Martin Buber, *The Way of Response* (New York: Schocken, 1966), 55.

[10]Ronald C. Arnett, "A Dialogic Ethic 'Between' Buber and Levinas: A Responsive Ethical I," in *Dialogue: Theorizing Difference in Communication Studies*, eds. Rob Anderson, Leslie A. Baxter, and Kenneth N. Cissna (Thousand Oaks, CA: Sage Publications, 2004), 79.

[11]Martin Buber, *Meetings: Autobiographical Fragments* (New York: Routledge, 2002), 22.

[12]Maurice Friedman, *Martin Buber's Life and Work* (Detroit: Wayne State University Press, 1988), 5.

[13]*Supra* note 11 at 22-3.

[14]Mona DeKoven Fishbane, "I, Thou, We: A Dialogical Approach to Couples Therapy," *Journal of Marital and Family Therapy* 24, no. 1 (1998): 41-58.

[15]Ibid., 55.

[16]Elliot R. Wolfson, "The Problem of Unity in the Thought of Martin Buber," *Journal of the History of Philosophy* 27, no. 3 (1989): 441-2.

[17]Maurice Friedman, "Martin Buber and Mikhail Bakhtin: The Dialogue of Voices and the Word That Is Spoken," *Religion and Literature* 33, no. 3 (2001): 25-36.

[18]*Supra* note 1 at 3.

[19]Michael Holquist, *Dialogism: Bakhtin and His World*, ed. Terrence Hawks (New York: Routledge, 1990).

[20]Ibid., 16.

[21]Ibid., 22.

[22]Ibid., 23.

[23]Mikhail Bakhtin, *Toward a Philosophy of the Act* (Austin: University of Texas Press, 1993), 38.

[24]Mikhail Bakhtin, *Speech Genres and Other Late Essays*, ed. Caryl Emerson and Michael Holquist (Austin: University of Texas Press, 1986), 72.

[25]Ibid., 75-6.

[26]*Supra* note 19 at 38.

[27]Alan Jacobs, *A Theology of Reading—The Hermeneutics of Love* (Cambridge: Westview Press, 2001), 51.

[28]*Supra* note 19 at 38.

[29]*Supra* note 23 at 38.

[30]Ibid.

[31]Ibid.

[32]Jo Sprague, Douglas Stuart, and David Bodary, *The Speaker's Handbook*, 9th ed. (Boston: Wadsworth, Cengage Learning, 2010).

[33]Etienne Gilson, *Reason and Revelation in the Medieval Ages* (New York: Scribner, 1963).

∞∞∞∞∞∞∞∞∞∞∞∞∞∞∞∞∞∞∞∞∞∞

References

"Founding Document." University Core Theme Area (2008-09).

Arnett, Ron C., Celeste Grayson, and Christy McDowell. "Dialogue as an Enlarged Communicative Mentality: Review Assessment and Ongoing Difference." Communication Research Trends 27, no. 3 (2008): 3-25.

Arnett, Ronald C. "A Dialogic Ethic 'Between' Buber and Levinas: A Responsive Ethical I." In *Dialogue: Theorizing Difference in Communication Studies.* Edited by Rob Anderson, Leslie A. Baxter, and Kenneth N. Cissna. Thousand Oaks, CA: Sage Publications, 2004.

Bakhtin, Mikhail. *Speech Genres and Other Late Essays.* Edited by Caryl Emerson and Michael Holquist. Austin: University of Texas Press, 1986.

———. *Toward a Philosophy of the Act.* Austin: University of Texas Press, 1993.

Buber, Martin. *Meetings: Autobiographical Fragments.* New York: Routledge, 2002.

———. *The Letters of Martin Buber: A Life of Dialogue.* Syracuse: Syracuse University Press, 1996.

———. *The Way of Response.* New York: Schocken, 1966.

Carrell, Lori J. "Diversity in the Communication Curriculum: Impact on Student Empathy." *Communication Education* 46, no. 1 (1997): 234-44.

Cissna, Kenneth N. and Rob Anderson. "Communication and the Ground of Dialogue." In *The Reach of Dialogue: Confirmation, Voice, and Community.* Edited by Rob Anderson, Kenneth N. Cissna, and Ronald C. Arnett. Cresskill, NJ: Hampton Press, 1994.

Fishbane, Mona DeKoven. "I, Thou, We: A Dialogical Approach to Couples Therapy," *Journal of Marital and Family Therapy* 24, no. 1 (1998): 41-58.

Friedman, Maurice. "Martin Buber and Mikhail Bakhtin: The Dialogue of Voices and the Word That Is Spoken." *Religion and Literature* 33, no. 3 (2001): 25-36.

———. *Martin Buber: The Life of Dialogue.* New York: Routledge, 2002.

———. *Martin Buber's Life and Work.* Detroit, MI: Wayne State University Press,

1988.

Gilson, Etienne. *Reason and Revelation in the Medieval Ages.* New York: Scribner, 1963.

Holquist, Michael. *Dialogism: Bakhtin and His World.* Edited by Terrence Hawks. New York: Routledge, 1990.

Jacobs, Alan. *A Theology of Reading—The Hermeneutics of Love.* Cambridge: Westview Press, 2001.

Johannesen, Richard. "The Emerging Concept of Communication as Dialogue." *Quarterly Journal of Speech* 57, no. 4 (1971): 373-82.

Lipari, Lisbeth. "Listening for the Other: Ethical Implications of the Buber-Levinas Encounter." *Communication Theory* 14, no. 2 (2004): 122-41.

Silberstein, Laurence J. "Martin Buber: The Social Paradigm in Modern Jewish Thought." *Journal of the American Academy of Religion* 49, no. 2 (1981): 211-29.

Sprague, Jo, Douglas Stuart, and David Bodary. *The Speaker's Handbook.* Boston: Wadsworth Cengage Learning, 2010.

Wolfson, Elliot R. "The Problem of Unity in the Thought of Martin Buber." *Journal of the History of Philosophy* 27, no. 3 (1989): 419-39.

Chapter 8

BODIES AT PEACE IN THE MOMENT OF DIALOGUE

Kenneth R. Chase

Agree to Disagree

The first World Parliament of Religion was held in Chicago on September 11, 1893, in the building that today stands as the Art Institute of Chicago. One of the most influential speakers at that august gathering was Swami Vivekananda, who spoke movingly of his Hinduism: "I am proud to belong to a religion which has taught the world both tolerance and universal acceptance. We believe not only in universal toleration, but we accept all religions as true." If one agrees with Swami Vivekananda, then one has a powerful basis for urging interfaith dialogue as the means through which those of differing religious beliefs can find common ground and shared goals. If, indeed, all religions are true and there will be no divine sorting at the end of time, then interfaith communication is a valuable process for overcoming the errors of exclusivist religion. Swami Vivekananda closed his 1893 speech:

> Sectarianism, bigotry, and its horrible descendant, fanaticism, have long possessed this beautiful earth. They have filled the earth with violence, drenched it often and often with human blood, destroyed civilization and sent whole nations to despair. . . . But their time is come; and I fervently hope that the bell that tolled this morning in honor of this convention may be the death-knell of all fanaticism, of all persecutions with the sword or with the pen, and of all uncharitable feelings between persons wending their way to the same goal.[1]

As Swami Vivekananda looked to the close of the nineteenth century, the approach of a more peaceful era was in his sight. He was wrong, of course. So, when Jitish Kallat reproduces this speech in his September 11, 2010, installation at the Art Institute of Chicago, he must acknowledge the irony of celebrating Swami Vivekananda's ideology in an era torn by religiously motivated hostilities. Kallat places the words of Swami Vivekananda's speech on the risers of the grand staircase in the institute's lobby, and each word is illuminated according to one of five different colors within the U.S. Homeland Security Advisory System, now discontinued. Kallat's "Public Notice 3" is not at all cynical; on the contrary, it evokes the 9/11 violence of religious fanaticism to call forth a renewal to the pluralism of which Swami Vivekananda speaks. These are old words, but Kallat sharpens them in the context of today's threats. Museum visitors not only see the multicolored evocation of Hindu universalism, they walk upon it as they move into the exhibits; the Swami's speech underlies the footsteps—and perhaps even the hopes—of today's urban aesthetes.[2]

As a Christian, I readily embrace Vivekananda's desire for peace, yet I cannot accept his sentiment that we achieve this peace by accepting all religions as equally true or that the pursuit of a universal religion provides peace's best hope. I am not alone in resisting Vivekananda's universalist beliefs, for the religious doctrines of the other Abrahamic monotheisms—Judaism and Islam—also deny the Hindu claim that all religions are equally true. Right out of the gate, the goal of achieving peace through a shared commitment to universal truth stumbles. Kallat's installation powerfully brings to mind the reality of deeply held religious differences, which cannot be wished away by a belief in pan-religious commonalities. A tragic fact of 9/11 is that religious exclusivists can reach fanatical extremes when they abandon the central moral tenets of their faith and pursue an aggressive hatred toward others. Although the terrorists of 9/11 have no serious claim to be faithfully Muslim, Kallat's art (perhaps unintentionally) exposes the very real religious tensions that make Swami Vivekananda's 19th century words seem like 21st century fiction. Those espousing interfaith dialogue cannot presume that those adherents holding exclusively to a single religion will alter their views. Rather, our practices of interfaith dialogue must match the ongoing reality of insurmountable religious difference. The purpose of interfaith dialogue must shift from the false hopes of universal agreement to something more realistic (but still exceedingly difficult), namely, the goal of living together peacefully while preserving fundamental religious difference. Rabbi Jonathan Sacks sees this shift as a necessary corrective to the dominant view within Western civilization over the past two millennia. The task for religious dialogue is not to reduce religions to their lowest common denominator, but to resist the quest for commonality and embrace the reality of difference.[3]

We are familiar with the cliché that to get along with those different from us we need to "agree to disagree." I support this old adage as valuable for the interfaith work that needs to happen to advance peace in our time. Yet, I disagree with many when it comes to explaining how we practice the "agree" part of the formula. When we communication scholars urge that communication be the central process for finding that point where religious exclusivists agree to disagree, we too often think of communication as verbal, as a meeting of minds in which thoughts are shared and beliefs are reconciled. So, for instance, Wayne Booth, the esteemed professor emeritus of English at the University of Chicago, sees "genuine listening" as crucial for the peaceful engagement of "Christians and Muslims; Catholics and Protestants; Mormons and Baptists; . . . Darwinists and creationists; postmodernist academics and traditionalists."[4] He describes this form of dialogue as a deep "probing for common ground" in which "both sides are pursuing not just victory but a new reality, a new agreement about what is real."[5] His ideal rests on a view of verbal practice: using words to advance more words and finding within those words new words that are mutually internalized. This is a pleasing sentiment for many interfaith gatherings, but is far from helpful in the toughest of interfaith challenges. The crucial starting point for interfaith encounters among those holding to exclusive religious beliefs is located not in the pursuit of agreed upon ideas or meanings, but at the level of the human body, at the level of being physically present with one another. This physical co-presence, even in the midst of deeply divisive religious disagreements, does not depend upon the discovery of some new reality or religious insight. It does not depend on the sharing of minds. It depends, rather, on the (non-verbal) agreement that letting each other live is preferable to participating in a global civilization terrorized by killing. Therefore, when religious exclusivists "agree to disagree" in the midst of violent cultural struggles, they must first agree at the non-verbal level; they must face each other in physical proximity—present before each other in the fullness of their human embodiment such that they are vulnerable to the other's judgment and yet strong enough to clasp hands and to sit together.

I have gleaned this lesson from Canon Andrew White, a highly celebrated mediator of interfaith gatherings throughout the Mideast. Canon White certainly encourages interfaith understanding and genuine listening as important for the work of peace; he urges that religious enemies understand each other's "culture, religion, traditions, and everything that shapes their expectations."[6] He, however, sees a more basic process of human engagement as primary, and this engagement takes seriously the role of the human body in forming relationships of peace.

Holding Hands and Sitting Close

As an Anglican priest serving as the vicar at Saint George's Church in Baghdad, Canon Andrew White focuses his current interfaith activities on Iraq. Over the past dozen years, though, he has guided interfaith dialogues throughout the Mideast. Canon White has been on the frontlines of Israeli-Palestinian conflicts and in the meeting rooms of the highest political and religious leaders of that conflicted region. His current work in Iraq is esteemed in the eyes of all. The price on his head and the more than two dozen Iraqi soldiers serving as bodyguards for his travels to and from Saint George's Church affirm that his interfaith efforts have impact for good against forces of evil. In some of the most challenging interfaith contexts of our time, Canon White seeks peaceful reconciliation. He engages this work without compromising his distinctive Christian convictions, nor does he ask Sunni or Shi'a Muslims to compromise theirs.

Prior to his work in Iraq, Canon White was mediator for the historic "First Alexandria Declaration of the Religious Leaders of the Holy Land."[7] It is in that context in which we find a kernel insight that pushes us to see the practices of peace in ways that reaffirm our best judgments about dialogue, but also refines that judgment according to the role of human bodies in the dialogic process. In a 2003 interview, Canon White describes the unique challenge of interfaith dialogue among Jewish and Palestinian leaders in that violence-fraught region:

> For me, the kind of relationships I have with other faith leaders is so different from what happens in the interfaith world. I often say that most interfaith gatherings are nice people sitting down talking with nice people. Well, most of my work begins with fairly horrible people sitting down talking to horrible people, horrible because they are caught up in some kind of war. Or they might not be horrible people—they might be very nice people—but they are still people who are hurting, people who are broken by violence—often very, very intense violence. So in my work, there is always a very specific objective, not just, "Let's sit down and be nice to each other," but "how do we stop killing each other?" It is very different from what people may consider an interfaith encounter. You know, this isn't cucumber sandwiches and cups of tea on the mayor's lawn, which is so often how these interfaith activities happen. These are hard-core negotiations trying to stop people killing, literally massacring, each other.[8]

Since leaders from Islam, Judaism, and Christianity all lay claim to Palestine, the task of forming any sort of productive dialogue is difficult, even more so the task of finding a hopeful resolution to the process. The primary emphasis in this sort of dialogue is meeting together, face-to-face, body-to-body. Of course, mutual understanding remains crucial, yet the impetus for the hard work of dialogic understanding begins with the mutual recognition that each other wants to stop the killing. "Stop killing me" becomes the first move of the dialogic process; it is the fundamental appeal that characterizes the initial approach of one person to another.

This initial recognition need not be spoken directly, for the fact that the conflicted parties are placing their bodies before each other is a nonverbal appeal to let peace reign, at least for this moment. By being physically present, each dialogic participant is vulnerable to death; yet each participant also has the capacity to demonstrate self-control and the strength of principled action in letting the interfaith partner live. This is the dialogic dance of frail human bodies—easily broken yet capable of physical control on behalf of others. Such interfaith dialogue displays both physical strength and physical weakness. "These are people who are hurting, people who are broken by violence," White explains. "One of the key characteristics [of dialogue] is to enable each side to hear the pain of the other . . . . [a]ctually listen and hear and emphasize and understand the pain of the other." White notes, however, that hearing the pain often can become competitive, with each party seeking to outdo the other with the depth of their suffering. This sort of conversation does not glimpse peace. Rather, it deepens the motivation to retreat from dialogue and find strength in the community of like-minded adherents, people who may seek to overcome weakness through killing. Interfaith dialogue must do more than merely foster the commonality of physical pain, for then participants in their face-to-face encounter become *nothing but* weak and vulnerable and seek to find their strength not through resolute acts of peace but through the warring sentiment of their own people. Interfaith participants also must have the physical capacity to assist others, to provide for, and to shield, if necessary. It is this mix of weakness and strength, of vulnerability and power, that makes the co-presence of human bodies vital to the dialogue process.

In a poignant anecdote pulled from part of the overall Alexandria process, Canon White provides a glimpse into the nature of embodied dialogue:

> This is the key—how to break that cycle of the competition of pain. It comes when there is a real encounter with the other and when the other stops becoming an enemy, but a friend. I often give the example of two of the key people I work with, Rabbi Michael Melchior, the former deputy from our ministry for Israel, our chief rabbi, the rabbi of Norway actually, and Sheik [sic] Tal El Sader [sic].

> Sheik Tal El Sader, a sheik from Hebron, former Minister of State within the Palestinian Authority [and founding member of Hamas], . . . was being totally and utterly bombarded by the Arab press at a meeting one day. After just sitting and listening to all of this for a while, he took Rabbi

Melchior's hand and said, "Rabbi Melchior is my brother. He is not my friend, he is my brother, and we are going to walk this long and difficult road together until we find peace together. And eventually, we will, because," he said, "my job is to pull up the thorns along this difficult road and to plant flowers."[9]

Canon White's account reveals both the weakness and the strength of these two religious leaders. Sheikh Tal El Sadr gives of his physical strength (both literally and figuratively) to hold, to walk, and to pull up thorns. This is his offer of service to Rabbi Melchior. Simultaneously, Sheikh Tal El Sadr depends on the strength of Rabbi Melchior to share the journey, reaching for the rabbi's hand to find assistance. Their task of interfaith dialogue is not to set aside their deep faith convictions in favor of some universal religion; rather, they seek merely to live peaceably with each other in a physical co-presence based not on the agreement of their thoughts but on the proximity of their bodies. Rabbi Melchior and Sheikh Tal El Sadr choose to walk along each other's side, knowing that one's own weakness requires the grasp of a hand, a hand that becomes a source of strength for the ongoing work of peaceful negotiation.

Canon White's more recent reconciliation work in Iraq gives us another perspective on the vital role of human embodiment at the center of any interfaith dialogue. Early in 2008, while suicide bombings, murders, and kidnappings were still a frequent feature of Iraqi life, Canon White convened an interfaith conference in Copenhagen involving a broad range of religious and political delegates from Iraq. The Danish government funded this Iraqi Reconciliation Conference to good end; the delegates produced a "strong statement" with a "detailed vision for the future of Iraq."[10] A month later, a follow-up meeting took place in Cairo featuring a select group of eighteen religious delegates from the highest levels of Iraq's Sunni and Shi'a communities. They, too, issued a strong statement that "announced a total rejection of all violence."[11] In describing this process, Canon White highlights the physical co-presence vital to interfaith agreements:

> As well as the formal outcomes of such meetings, however, the informal business that goes on between sessions is just as important. On the last

evening, we were crammed into a small bus on our way to a final meal together when one of the Sunni sheikhs started singing a Sunni religious song and one by one the others joined in. When Ayatollah Abu Ragif [senior lieutenant of Grand Ayatollah al-Sistani] asked them to sing a Shia song, there was a moment of tension before they obliged and then everyone, Sunni and Shia, began laughing and singing.[12]

It was the crowded bus, the intensity of the bodies pressed together, that provided a context for mutual support. The tension of disagreement—involving leaders of rival sects embedded in centuries of animosity—is pressed into the service of shared song and laughter through physical closeness.

It is always this way in Canon White's work. Peacemaking in the midst of religious violence demands the hard work of building relationships through frequent face-to-face contact. Canon White's experiences give us a glimpse into this moment of peace between persons. He emphasizes that "we need to find a way to keep people moving along [the road to reconciliation]," and this "may involve arranging regular conferences, seminars or private meetings between religious and political leaders, or it may mean something more informal, such as a meal together."[13] Any sustained reflection on the horrors of ethnic, political, and religious violence teaches us that we must cherish those moments when bodies are at peace.

We ought to pause then on Canon White's distinctive role as interfaith peacemaker. White does not presume that his process provides any guaranteed results or that the mystery of interfaith tolerance will be finally solved. In celebrating Canon White's interfaith work, I only claim that the type of embodied interaction he models is precisely what we need if we are to survive with each other in the face of insurmountable differences. This is no recipe for agreement or for complete and enduring peace. It is, rather, a vital element of our attempt to simply get along. If Abrahamic exclusivists are to "agree to disagree," then a large part of what they "agree" upon is the baseline preference—conveyed through physical co-presence—that religious monotheists prefer not to be killed or to be the killers. As long as they are meeting in an interfaith process—face-to-face and body-to-body—they are practicing co-existence in proximity. If we extend the process and expand the number of participants, we are glimpsing the possibility of peace. Given the millennia-old struggles of religious conflict, enacting any sort of temporary glimpse is cause for grateful celebration. These are the moments we reflect upon, seeking ways to continue the temporary peace, perhaps for months and years to come.

Why is the co-presence of human bodies crucial for interfaith work? To answer this question, we need to move beyond a notion of dialogue that views communication merely as the sharing of meanings through the exchange of symbols. Communication is not a tool that humans pull from their bag of resources, as if the right words will make everything better, but a process of living together through which humans shape identities, relationships, and communities. As such, it is an ethical process involving practices of peace and violence, mercy and hate, justice and revenge. By looking more closely at the theory and philosophy of human dialogue, therefore, we gain a deeper level of insight into how the seemingly simple communicative acts of holding hands or sharing the same bus seat become significant interfaith events.

Facing Peace

Two of the most significant thinkers on the nature of dialogue are Martin Buber and Emmanuel Levinas. As European Jews shaped by the world wars of the twentieth century, Buber and Levinas craft powerful visions of ethical interaction, particularly the practices of peace and their violation. For Levinas, peace is violated when one person assimilates the other person.[14] This is the holocaust on a small scale, the one-by-one annihilation of others through one's own ego-centric projects.[15] When we torture or kill the body, we are violently submitting others to our will. We also can do this type of violence with language; by using hate speech, stereotyping, or manipulative debate tactics, we reduce and deny others in a verbal attempt to gain submission. Violence, whether verbal or nonverbal, occurs when we treat others exclusively as means for our own ends.

Martin Buber describes this utilitarian practice as an I-It relation. Although Buber insists that we need I-It relations in order to survive in this world (we must consider other people at times for what they

do for us, such as provide medical care, food, shelter, encouragement, emotional and spiritual support), he insists that I-It relations
ought not be the *only* relations we have. Rather, we ought to be always open to non-utilitarian relations with others, those moments of
grace where we live an I-Thou relation and, hence, participate in the
fullness of social communion.[16] Violence emerges when the I-Thou
is disintegrated and the I-It dimension of our experience becomes
"gigantically swollen"; in a fully utilitarian mode of living, the truly
peaceful and ethical relationship among persons is absent.[17] Thus, the
simple acts of handholding and sitting close together are, philosophi-
cally speaking, not so simple.

In the instances Canon White has described, handholding and
sitting close are powerful gestures of mutual personhood that place
partnership above egocentricity. Of course, sometimes a person may
grab another's hand or violate personal space in a way that establishes
hierarchy and a fully utilitarian I-It relation. But this is not handholding, it is hand grabbing, and this is not sitting close, it is intrusion—
these acts participate in the violence of assimilation. Handholding
or sitting close are side by side, a mutual grasp or a shared space that
both gives and receives strength, and that admits the neediness and
weakness of the solitary individual.

Levinas has something more to teach us about peace and violence
in dialogue, though. We act violently when we assimilate others to
our own interests, yet we also can treat ourselves violently when we
collapse both self and others into a common ideal of unity, reason,
or knowledge. Levinas is suspicious, then, of those models of dialogue that promote shared meanings and common ideas as a way of
peace. He argues this type of dialogue is a subtly violent reduction
of self and others into a molded conformity. In this flawed model of
peace, our differences are treated as problems to be solved through
the pursuit of overarching sameness.[18] From Levinas's vantage point,
Swami Vivekananda's speech guides us not toward peace but toward
the assimilation of monotheistic religions into a universal religious
sentiment. To claim that all religions are true is to reduce them all to
mere expressions of the larger religious truth, which in the swami's
speech is his version of Hinduism.

Levinas and Buber reject a model of dialogue that treats self and others as means to the end of an all-encompassing conformity.[19] For both Buber and Levinas, dialogue is a type of peaceful sociality that cannot be collapsed into a bundle of shared meanings or into a quest for unified knowledge. Dialogue, rather, is the place where the face-to-face meeting evokes a sense of responsibility for others without reducing them to one's own or someone else's ideas. In truly peaceful dialogue, we face each other and become aware that our understanding is limited. We reach out to offer and receive assistance in making our way through a hard and painful world.

Tension and Difference

In the face-to-face interfaith dialogue, human bodies are involved, not just the meanings of religious teachings or the ideologies of warring politics. To live peacefully in this moment is to be vulnerable, to see the eyes and hands and flesh of the other person. John Stewart and Karen Zediker describe these peaceful interactions as involving multiple interconnected "tensions." At the center of all these animating forces is the primary tension between a dialogue participant "holding my own ground" and simultaneously "letting the other happen to me."[20] In ethical dialogue, claim Stewart and Zediker, we must speak from our own convictions and experiences (holding ground) while also receiving what the other participants contribute from their convictions and experiences (letting be). Having a dialogue within this tension is to foster an I-Thou relationship. There is no reduction of others to my own agenda, nor a loss of my own convictions to some overarching ideal of unified religious truth. We do not hope for some magic agreement that will make our differences disappear. Rather, we agree to see each other, to travel far so that the fragments of a relationship can be put together, to clasp hands with each other, and to sit close by in the midst of palpable differences. This is the tension of being generous in giving our own convictions and being hospitable in receiving the convictions of others.

Navigating interpersonal tensions through physical co-presence is only a starting point for the more extended verbal interactions by which interfaith discussants hold their ground and welcome other beliefs; yet, these peaceful moments of touch, sight, and smell provide an ideal achievement in their own right. In his comprehensive survey of the term *communication* in American history, John Durham Peters exposes the unrealistic dreams shaping the view that verbal communication is an answer to our conflicting differences. We are nurturing a false hope, he argues, if we cling to the ideal that people can deeply and authentically understand each other, as if we can achieve a common mind through more effective communication. The chasms of understanding that divide religious faiths are frustratingly present in all human language use, not just interfaith conversations. We live amidst gaps in meanings—never fully comprehending the inner life of those around us, including our closest intimates, and never fully being understood by others.

Given this deeply human condition, Peters urges us to place priority not on shared meanings but on "the successful coordination of behavior."[21] By giving up the dream of our minds melding into common agreement, Peters claims we free ourselves to pursue the far more important relational practice of caring for one another in the midst of our differences. He explains, "The question should be not Can we communicate with each other? but *Can we love one another or treat each other with justice and mercy?*"[22] As interfaith participants face each other with disagreements so deep that the meeting is crippled through frustrations and resentments, then the participants must be merciful, forgiving themselves and others for the human frailties that produce such division. In this glimpse of mutual weakness, participants can continue the dialogue. When interfaith meetings enable participants to reach toward one another in peaceful proximity— not in the attempt to eliminate tensions but to act mercifully within them—then these are successful communicative achievements.

Building on Difference

In the toughest interfaith contexts, the participants often do not meet the ideal of mutual support, mercy, or caring service. Writing in 2005, Canon White describes the challenges he faces in Mideast peacemaking: "If [inter-religious dialogue] is really to bear fruit, it must include those who are generally regarded as the greatest exponents of violence. On the whole, 'nice' people do not cause wars, and so if inter-religious activity involves only nice people talking to nice people it will be futile."[23] Nice people try to listen and understand; some of the people killing each other in today's Iraq are not the listening types. Canon White has discovered that many of the techniques typically recommended for interfaith peacemaking simply do not work in this context: "established strategies for resolving conflict—working through political issues, restoring civil society, supporting the moderates, involving women—are mostly ineffectual."[24] His alternative practice is on relationship building with the leaders of the monotheistic faiths. This is the process requiring physical proximity; it demands an ongoing effort to place people, divided by religious conflict, into the same physical space.

As an ingredient in the larger-scale pursuit of peace within the Mideast, interfaith dialogue allows the leaders of monotheistic faiths to sit down together, face-to-face, and for a moment practice the peace that they are seeking to achieve for all members of their communities. Canon White often says, "If religion is part of the problem, it must be part of the solution."[25] For Canon White himself, his devotion to Christ is what propels him to seek the well-being of his Muslim and Jewish neighbors. His particular motivation differs, of course, from those Muslim and Jewish leaders with whom he pursues relationships, yet they too have faith-motivated reasons to make embodied relationships the starting point of their dialogues for peace.

Canon White offers us a realistic appraisal of the toughest interfaith conversations. His insight, though, is not limited to those tough cases. All dialogues can benefit from his simple truth made rich through philosophical reflection and theoretical analysis: The goal of interfaith dialogue is not to overcome differences through some grand agreement, but to celebrate peaceful co-presence in the midst of those differences. This is the path toward reconciliation. This is the path faith adherents follow when they meet with others, even their enemies, and in a single tension-filled moment reach out not to kill but to live.

◇◇◇◇◇◇◇◇◇◇◇◇◇◇◇◇◇◇◇◇◇◇◇◇◇◇◇◇◇◇◇◇

Notes

[1]Swami Vivekananda's speech is available online through the Art Institute of Chicago, http://www.artic.edu/aic/collections/resource/1082.

[2]For additional information and analysis of Kallat's art and a valuable review of Swami Vivekananda's contributions to the Parliament, see Madhuvanti Ghose, ed. *Jitish Kallat: Public Notice* 3 (Chicago: The Art Institute of Chicago, 2011).

[3]Jonathan Sacks, *The Dignity of Difference: How to Avoid the Clash of Civilizations* (London: Continuum, 2002), 48.

[4]Wayne C. Booth, *The Rhetoric of Rhetoric: The Quest for Effective Communication* (Malden, MA: Blackwell, 2004), 149.

[5]Ibid., 47.

[6]Andrew White, *The Vicar of Baghdad: Fighting for Peace in the Middle East* (Oxford, UK: Monarch Books, 2009), 123.

[7]For further information about the Alexandria Declaration and a complete copy, see, e.g., the website of Mosaica's Center for Inter-Religious Cooperation, http://www.mosaica-interreligious.org. Western press coverage of the declaration and the surrounding dialogue was surprisingly sparse or nonexistent. For general notices, see J. Brilliant, "Religious Summit Calls for Peace," United Press Syndicate, January 21, 2002, accessed July 15, 2006, from LexisNexis; and T. Jones, "Religious Heads in Mid East [sic] Peace Talks," Press Association, October 2002, accessed July 15, 2006, from LexisNexis. For Canon White's account of the overall process, see White, *supra* note 6 at 21-41; for his most recent reflections on this process, see his *Faith Under Fire* (Oxford, UK: Monarch Books, 2011), 30-31. For additional information about White and his ongoing work with interfaith dialogue, see, Kim Lawton, "Interview: Canon Andrew White," February 3, 2006, accessed August 28, 2011, from http://www.pbs.org/wnet/religionandethics/week923/interview.html; and Canon White's Foundation for Reconciliation in the Middle East website, at www.frme.org.

[8]Kenneth R. Chase, "Canon Andrew White Interview," Center for Applied Christian Ethics, October 16, 2003, accessed August 28, 2011, from http://www.wheaton.edu/CACE/CACE-Print-Resources.

[9]Ibid.; n.p. White also recounts this story in, *supra* note 6 at 40.

[10]*Supra* note 6 at 108.

[11]Ibid.

[12]Ibid., 108-9.

[13]Ibid., 129.

[14]In this brief exposition of Levinas's insight into violence and dialogue, I have avoided his technical philosophical vocabulary in favor of paraphrasing

that draws similarities between his thought, Martin Buber's, and general theory on dialogic communication. Levinas's philosophy has shaped my orientation to Canon White's practice, yet any precise statement of this connection exceeds the bounds of this chapter. One technical element I have avoided—but worth noting for its applicability to my argument about dialogue—is the convention among Levinas's translators to capitalize the term *Other*, which emphasizes the fullness of the ethical responsibility we have toward other persons and the sort of honor we give to other persons as we approach them in the embodied relationship of peace.

[15]Emmanuel Levinas, *Totality and Infinity*, trans. Alphonso Lingis (Pittsburgh: Duquesne University Press, 1969). One of the best introductions to Levinas's thought is his *Ethics and Infinity: Conversations with Philippe Nemo*, trans. Richard A. Cohen (Pittsburgh: Duquesne University Press, 1985).

[16]Martin Buber, *I and Thou*, trans. Walter Kaufmann (New York: Charles Scribner's, 1970), 97-8.

[17]Martin Buber, "Replies to My Critics," in *The Philosophy of Martin Buber*, eds. Paul Arthur Schlipp and Maurice Friedman (La Salle: Open Court, 1967), 715.

[18]Emmanuel Levinas, *Of God Who Comes to Mind*, trans. Bettina Bergo (Stanford, CA: Stanford University Press, 1998), 141.

[19]E.g., Ibid., 143.

[20]John Stewart and Karen E. Zediker, "Dialogue as Tensional, Ethical Practice," *Southern Communication Journal* 65 (2000): 224-42.

[21]John Durham Peters, *Speaking into the Air: A History of the Idea of Communication* (Chicago: University of Chicago Press, 1999), 268.

[22]Ibid. (emphasis added).

[23]Andrew White, *Iraq: Searching for Hope* (London: Continuum, 2005), 96.

[24]White, *supra* note 6 at 123.

[25]Ibid., 137.

Bibliography

Booth, Wayne C. *The Rhetoric of Rhetoric: The Quest for Effective Communication.* Malden, MA: Blackwell, 2004.

Buber, Martin. *I and Thou.* Translated by Walter Kaufmann. New York: Charles Scribner's, 1970.

———. "Replies to My Critics." In *The Philosophy of Martin Buber.* Edited by Paul Arthur Schlipp and Maurice Friedman. La Salle: Open Court, 1967.

Brilliant, Joshua. "Religious Summit Calls for Peace," United Press Syndicate, January 21, 2002, accessed July 15, 2006.

Canon White's Foundation for Reconciliation in the Middle East. www.frme.org.

Chase, Kenneth R. "Canon Andrew White Interview." Center for Applied Christian Ethics, October 16, 2003, accessed August 28, 2011.

Ghose, Madhuvanti. *Jitish Kallat: Public Notice 3.* Edited by Madhuvanti Ghose. Chicago: The Art Institute of Chicago, 2011.

Jones, T. "Religious Heads in Mid East [sic] Peace Talks," Press Association, October 2002, accessed July 15, 2006.

Lawton, Kim. *Interview: Canon Andrew White.* February 3, 2006, accessed August 28, 2011.

Levinas, Emmanuel. *Ethics and Infinity: Conversations with Philippe Nemo.* Translated by Richard A. Cohen. Pittsburgh: Duquesne University Press, 1985.

———. *Of God Who Comes to Mind.* Translated by Bettina Bergo. Stanford, CA: Stanford University Press, 1998.

———. *Totality and Infinity.* Translated by Alphonso Lingis. Pittsburgh: Duquesne University Press, 1969.

Mosaica's Center for Inter-Religious Cooperation. http://www.mosaica-interreligious.org.

Peters, John Durham. *Speaking into the Air: A History of the Idea of Communication.* Chicago: University of Chicago Press, 1999.

Sacks, Jonathan. *The Dignity of Difference: How to Avoid the Clash of Civilizations.* London: Continuum, 2002.

Stewart, John and Karen E. Zediker. "Dialogue as Tensional, Ethical Practice." *Southern Communication Journal* 65 (2000): 224-42.

Vivekananda, Swami. "Speech at the Art Institute of Chicago." http://www.artic.edu/aic/collections/resource/1082.

White, Andrew. *Faith Under Fire.* Oxford: Monarch Books, 2011.

———. *Iraq: Searching for Hope.* London: Continuum, 2005.

———. *The Vicar of Baghdad: Fighting for Peace in the Middle East.* Oxford: Monarch Books, 2009.

Chapter 9

Freedom of Speech, Communication, and Interfaith Dialogue: A Jewish Perspective

Tsuriel Rashi

◇◇◇◇◇◇◇◇◇◇◇◇◇◇◇◇◇◇◇◇◇◇◇◇◇◇◇◇◇◇◇◇◇

Humanity's Uniqueness as a Creature Having the Faculty of Speech

Because the basis of religious understanding depends on belief in a divine lawgiver, all-knowing and omnipotent, whose will and commandments are an obligation for eternity, religion and freedom of speech would seem to be contradictory and irreconcilable concepts. However, if we look at the overall approach to freedom of expression in the sources of Jewish Law, we find an impressive array of opinions, which, in itself, is evidence of a certain degree of freedom of expression. Within the general picture, there are different streams, sometimes overt and latent, side by side which together create a complex and intricate picture.

Judaism regards human beings as unique because they have the faculty of speech. Onkelos, in the second-century BCE Aramaic translation of the Bible that was used by the translators of the familiar King James Version, expressed this idea succinctly when he wrote about the creation of man: "And the Lord God formed man [of] the dust of the ground, and breathed into his nostrils the breath of life; and man became a living soul" (Genesis 2:7, KJV). In other words, "a speaking soul." Speech makes the person, and the faculty of speech is his breath of life.

Human beings have been given this faculty, but they are commanded to use it wisely. The Midrash, which is a homiletic method of biblical exegesis, points out that people are speaking creatures and that there is a human need to speak; it praises the unique beauty of speech, but also warns of the necessary restrictions on this faculty.[1] The Midrash first quotes the words of King Solomon in the Book of Proverbs: "Sin is not ended by multiplying words, but the prudent hold their tongues" (Prov. 10:19). The Midrash then explains, "He who refrains from talking about his friend is wise," and brings this homily to illustrate the point:

> Two philosophers debated the subject before the Emperor Hadrian. One claimed that speech was beautiful, whereas the other claimed that silence was golden. One of them said to the Emperor: "My Lord, there is nothing better than speech—were there no speech, how could brides be praised? How could there be negotiations in the world? How could boats set sail over the seas?"
>
> The Emperor turned immediately to the other one, who espoused the virtue of silence: "What do you have to say in defense of silence?"
>
> Before he even had the opportunity to respond, the one who was defending speech slapped him on the mouth.
>
> The Emperor said to him: "Why did you slap his face?" He replied: "My Lord, I defended speech using speech and he dares to defend his case using my instruments!"

The Midrash ends with this conclusion: "King Solomon said: God did not say that your mouth should be dumb and that you should sit in silence like a mute, but that 'you should restrain your lips and refrain from talking about your friend'—take heed to avoid punishment."

People are not expected to be mute but to be aware of every word they utter. Being careful about what one says is not synonymous with the absence of dialogue or dispute, and anyone who thinks so is sadly mistaken. This homily indicates that the faculty of speech that distinguishes humans from other creatures has the power to create globalization, which engages different cultures together and advances international shipping and commerce.

The Culture of Polemics and the Freedom of Opinion and Expression in the Bible

There are many biblical sources that deal with "the culture of polemics," which are evidence of the custom of public debate in Israel—in open dialogues with the Lord, between prophets or public leaders, or between the people.[2] All of this public debate is done by discussion, by airing grievances, complaints and requests, instructions and reservations, arguments, and so on. Examples of such episodes can be found in many places in the Bible and indicate that the culture of polemics was widespread in ancient Israel. Hence, we can find discussions between Moses and the nation or Moses and the Lord that reflect two opposing sides that have to talk, to persuade, and to reach mutual agreement whenever there is serious dissension between them. "Moses answered, 'What if they do not believe me or listen to me . . . ?'" (Exodus 4:1). Similarly, there are prophets and community leaders who discussed matters with the Lord and argued with him, beginning with Cain, who appealed against divine retribution. The patriarch Abraham fought for Sedom, and Job argued about the existence of divine justice in the Lord's world.

Across the generations, community leaders have conducted public debates with the nation, and they are documented in many places in the Bible: consider for instance, Joshua's discussion with the two-and-a-half tribes (Joshua 24), Gideon's dialogue with the people of Israel (Judges 18), Samuel's arguments with the people (1 Samuel 8), and the long, protracted public debate between Saul and the nation (1 Samuel 14). These are just a few of the many examples in the Bible demonstrating a way of thinking that encourages and promotes discussion and dialogue. These dialogues clearly do not settle for laconic statements, orders, or one-way instructions.

Sometimes these discussions in the Bible begin with a question that elicits a response or responses from one or more individuals in the group, such as "If you say to yourself" or "Do not say to yourself," among others (Deuteronomy 7:17; 8:17; 9:4). Against such a broad background of an ethos of discussion and dispute, it is hardly surprising that a culture of freedom of opinion and freedom of critical thought and freedom of speech developed.

Freedom of Opinion and Critical Thought: The Prophets as Role Models

Some commentators have suggested that the roots of freedom of expression in the Bible can be found in the Book of Numbers with Eldad and Medad, who prophesied in the camp. Unlike Joshua, who wanted to restrain them, Moses proposed granting them freedom of expression: "Joshua son of Nun, who had been Moses' aide since youth, spoke up and said, 'Moses, my lord, stop them!' but Moses replied, 'Are you jealous for my sake? I wish that all the Lord's people were prophets and that the Lord would put his Spirit on them!'" (Numbers 11:28-29). The Midrash on this passage tries to explain that these prophets foretold that Moses would die and that Joshua would lead the people of Israel into Canaan in his stead, which is why Joshua wanted to restrain them.

Those who contend that the right to freedom of speech can be found in Jewish Law find evidence for their claim in the books of the prophets. It is well known that those books are informative sources of sharp criticism of the actions of rulers as well as individuals: for example, "Your rulers are rebels, partners with thieves; they all love bribes and chase after gifts. They do not defend the cause of the fatherless; the widow's case does not come before them" (Isaiah 1:23). This freedom of expression often engendered the fury of the government, which sometimes was not satisfied with a strong verbal reaction and took harsh measures to suppress.[3]

Many commentators regard the prophets as the outspoken exponents of freedom of speech. The slogan for the prophetic rhetoric could well be this verse from Isaiah: "For Zion's sake I will not keep silent, for Jerusalem's sake I will not remain quiet. . ."[4] In other words, for the sake of a higher ideal, one must speak and not be still when the public welfare demands protest. Not holding one's peace is expected. The prophets certainly dared to berate the nation for its complacency, immorality, hypocrisy, and cruelty, but they were also not deterred by kings, priests, or ministers and were often imprisoned, tortured, and even murdered because they engaged in freedom of expression. This has been noted by Zechariah Chafee in *Freedom of Speech and Press:*

The most notable contribution of the Bible to the cause of freedom of speech is its portrayal of prophets and apostles who spoke out the truth that was in them without fear of consequences. Many an English and American agitator forced to face judges and officials has been deterred from timidity and capitulation by remembering Nathan excoriating David for putting Uriah the Hittite in the forefront of the battle, Elijah hunting out Ahab to denounce the lawless seizure of Naboth's vineyard. Like these men of old, dissenters have gone on talking and writing because they would rather be in prison or die then fail in their duty by keeping silent.[5]

One of the best examples of the prophets' struggle for freedom of expression appears in the Jeremiah 26, where Jeremiah prophesies that the Temple and Jerusalem will be destroyed. As a result, the nation wants him to leave, and the people want to hang him. At the last minute the elders of Judea stepped in and prevented the murder, and two precedents were invoked in the field trial that followed. The first tells of a prophet named Micah, who prophesied during the reign of King Hezekiah, and following his prophecy the king repented. The second refers to a prophet named Uriahu, who prophesied the destruction to King Jehoyakin. After his prophecy Uriahu escaped to Egypt, but soldiers were sent to bring him back to Jerusalem, where he was executed. At the end of his trial Jeremiah was set free but barely managed to escape the fury of the crowd.

It is sometimes argued that there is no legitimacy to a comparison between the words of the biblical prophets and contemporary freedom of expression because the prophets were transmitting the word of the Lord to the nation.[6] That being the case the prophet was not free to say whatever he thought, but had to speak the word of God exactly as it came to him, without additions or omissions. Furthermore, the prophecy was given specifically to that prophet, as Amos said, "I was neither a prophet nor the son of a prophet, but I was a shepherd, and I also took care of sycamore-fig trees. But the Lord took me from tending the flock and said to me, 'Go, prophesy to my people Israel.'"[7]

Nevertheless, it is possible to discern a culture of critical thought that often appears in the Bible. Clearly, there was no hesitation about criticizing rulers. In the Book of Kings we read that eleven of the nineteen kings of Judea did "what was evil in the eyes of the Lord." Only two, Hezekiah and Joshiahu, were considered righteous, and the remaining six were accorded only conditional commendation.[8] The nineteen kings of Israel fared far worse. Not one of them was viewed in an entirely positive light.

Even God, in all his glory, was not immune to criticism. Abraham and Moses, Jeremiah and Habakkuk, Job, and the poets of the Psalms did not hesitate to blame God on occasion. The inner strength that enabled them to criticize the Almighty came from a belief in the preeminence of justice and law to which even God must submit. Their harsh words were not censored in the canonic Bible in spite of the fact that they included strong criticisms of God. Moreover, it is even reasonable to say that God himself showed the importance of diversified discussion, since it was he who laid the foundations for the creation of diverse cultures when he dispersed the people as they were building the Tower of Babel.

The Tower of Babel, Interfaith Dialogue, and Freedom of Speech

As the world is made up of various cultures and religions, interfaith dialogue is a prime necessity. The very fact of such diversity is problematic from the beginning, since it would surely be preferable for all humanity to believe in one religion without dissension. Nonetheless, one nineteenth-century commentator analyzed the story of the Tower of Babel in terms of the importance of the creation of different cultures and their differential development. The Babel story can be considered foundational in connection with the issue of freedom of speech, especially as it was understood in the Jewish tradition, which combines core elements that underlie liberalism and social responsibility and is clearly antithetical to a totalitarian mindset.

The Tower of Babel narrative is the first story in the Bible that helps us to understand God's view concerning freedom of speech. The story opens with "The whole earth was of one language and of one speech."

Now the whole world had one language and a common speech. As people moved eastward, they found a plain in Shinar and settled there. They said to each other, "Come, let's make bricks and bake them thoroughly." They used brick instead of stone, and tar for mortar. Then they said, "Come, let us build ourselves a city, with a tower that reaches to the heavens, so that we may make a name for ourselves; otherwise we will be scattered over the face of the whole earth." But the Lord came down to see the city and the tower the people were building. The Lord said, "If as one people speaking the same language they have begun to do this, then nothing they plan to do will be impossible for them. Come, let us go down and confuse their language so they will not understand each other." So the Lord scattered them from there over all the earth, and they stopped building the city. That is why it was called Babel—because there the Lord confused the language of the whole world. From there the Lord scattered them over the face of the whole earth. (Genesis 11:1-9)

This short narrative raises a number of questions and thoughts: First, what is the significance of the fact that humanity does not speak only "one language" but also "one speech"? Second, why did those who wanted to build a tower "that reaches to the heavens" start building it in a valley and not on top of one of the mountains? Further, the Bible describes how God comes down to see "the city and the tower the people were building," but a few verses later God himself says "they have begun to do this, then nothing they plan to do will be impossible for them." Over and above these questions and beyond the story, we have this basic question: Why did God destroy the Tower of Babel? If they do no harm, why not leave them, and if they are sinners, why not kill them as he did in the great flood?

According to a unique biblical commentary by Rabbi Naftali Zvi Berlin at the beginning of the twentieth century, the answer is rooted in an understanding of this story of the Tower of Babel as the first Orwellian "Big Brother." According to Rabbi Berlin, the words "of one speech" bothered the Lord, as they signified homogeneity of thought and the lack of any opposition. Opposition became a normative prerequisite in Judaism for the proper functioning of society.

Moreover, the aspiration to build "a city, with a tower that reaches to the heavens, . . . otherwise we will be scattered over the face of the whole earth" is understood by Rabbi Berlin as what we understand today as an Orwellian "Big Brother" concept, whereby all are to be carefully observed from the tower constantly and are not allowed to leave their own settlement, lest they come into contact with others having different ideas.[9] Thus, it is not as megalomania-cal *building engineers* that they are punished by God but rather as totalitarian-minded *social engineers* who sought artificial and forced social consensus.

The purpose of the tower was to monitor and censor speech in the new city around it. This was what God opposed and why he de-stroyed the tower and the city: "If they will finish the building of the tower, they will be able to control the people and to avoid new ideas, and this is a thought that destroys the society and therefore there is no use in the fact that they are united right now."[10] Thus, the narra-tive points to a unique and unexpected attitude toward freedom of speech from a religious point of view.

The sixteenth-century book *Be'er Hagolah,* written by Rabbi Ju-dah Aryeh Loew, known to scholars of Judaism as the Maharal of Prague, condemned "silencing critics," even in the world of religious philosophy and the struggle against spurious opinions in "the free market" of opinions. The Maharal of Prague's insights and conten-tions, although expressed some 400 years ago, continue to be very valid in this day and age. In his preface, the Maharal quotes Aristotle, whose book *On the Heavens* deals with the proper way to conduct a dispute. According to Aristotle:

> Those who have first heard the pleas of our adversaries will be more likely
> to credit the assertions which we are going to make . . . To give a satisfac-
> tory decision as to the truth it is necessary to be rather an arbitrator than
> a party to the dispute.[11]

The Maharal supplements this, saying that what Aristotle says is correct not only for ordinary disputes but "that the words he wrote are true also for issues of belief." He even goes one step further, noting:

> In particular, when the person who dissented had no intention to annoy
> but merely to utter his belief (the truth), even if the things he has to say are

contrary to our belief one must not say to him, "don't talk and be silent," since there will be no clarification of the belief; on the contrary, this is what we should say, "say as much as you want and whatever you desire to say" and do not say, "if I had the opportunity to talk, I would say more" for he who does not allow another to talk, shows the weakness of his own belief.[12]

This quote from the Maharal is in line with the words of John Stuart Mill in the second chapter of his book *On Liberty:*

If to be obstructed in the enjoyment of it were simply a private injury, it would make some difference whether the injury was inflicted only on a few persons or on many. But the peculiar evil of silencing the expression of an opinion is that it is robbing the human race, posterity as well as the existing generation, those who dissent from the opinion, still more than those who hold it. If the opinion is right, they are deprived of the opportunity of exchanging error for truth: if wrong, they lose, what is almost as great a benefit, the clearer perception and livelier impression of truth, produced by its collision with error.[13]

The Maharal of Prague concludes with an allegory that illustrates how someone who wants to promote his belief must engage in a dialogue with a dissenter:

Every strong man who wants to dissent with another must find a worthy antagonist, hence should he be victorious, he is indeed the stronger of the two; but what does the strength show if his opponent is not capable of fighting against him? Certainly, if a master overcomes his servant, the master does not show any skill since the servant cannot, nor is he allowed to, fight against his master.[14]

Therefore, the Maharal adds his operative conclusions:

Hence it is not appropriate to reject the opinion of a dissenter, but it is appropriate to bring him closer, and to take note of his opinion . . . in this way a man approaches the true content of things and reaches the absolute truth. . . . so one must not silence a person who speaks against a belief, saying "do not speak like that"; on the contrary, whoever does so, shows his own weakness.[15]

The Maharal's theory is that especially those who want to strengthen their religious belief must hold a dialogue with the religion they are challenging. In the same way as a boxer who wants to win the world championship must challenge the world champion, the believer who wants to promote his belief in the labyrinth of religions must hold dialogues with other religions.[16]

∞∞∞∞∞∞∞∞∞∞∞∞∞∞∞∞∞∞∞∞∞∞∞∞

Conclusion

In a world where different cultures and religions are growing further apart ideologically, yet have never been closer technologically, it is particularly important to take account of the Aristotelian concept and translate it into an interfaith communicative discourse. If the human race is unique in having the faculty of speech, and if there is an imperative to use it to enter into discussion and engage in dialogue, then we should use it in the context of communication and religion. We must make every effort to promote interfaith discourse in the media while understanding the uniqueness of human beings as creatures who are able to speak and accept that critical thought is a moral beacon for their actions.

The Maharal introduced a radical Aristotelian idea to the world of religious philosophy, insisting on the necessity of dialogue even when the believer's natural instinct is to reject discourse with those he considers heretical. He argued that religious truth can only be clarified through interfaith dialogue. The same idea was echoed by John Stuart Mill in his praise for freedom of expression and freedom of the press. However, these ideas still await a resonant echo from the monotheistic religions.

The monotheistic religions, in particular, which share a common antecedent and have always acknowledged the contribution of the prophets to the fashioning of freedom of expression and freedom of thought, should, on the one hand, regard the differences between them as creative forces, and, on the other, promote the importance of interfaith discourse and mutual inspiration. The present volume of collected essays will perhaps turn out to be a significant milestone in the furtherance of these goals.

◇◇◇◇◇◇◇◇◇◇◇◇◇◇◇◇◇◇◇◇◇◇◇◇◇◇◇

Notes

[1]Shimon Ashkenazi, *Yalkut Shim'oni on the Torah* (Jerusalem: Jerusalem Institute, 2006), paragraph 737.

[2]For a review of arguments with the Lord in the Jewish heritage, see Anson Laytner, *Arguing with God: A Jewish Tradition* (Lanham, MD: Rowman & Littlefield, 1990).

[3]See, for example, 1 Kings 1:18. According to one tradition, King Menashe murdered the prophet Isaiah and the nation threw stones at Jeremiah. Echoes of this tradition are also found in the Talmud (Yebemoth, page 49, column 2).

[4]Isaiah 62:1.

[5]Zechariah Chafee, *Freedom of Speech and Press* (New York: Carrie Chapman Catt Memorial Fund, 1955), 15.

[6]After all the word "prophet" is an epithet for "the mouth of God." Cf. "I have put my words in your mouth" (Jeremiah 1: 9). Not for nothing is the prophet considered one who does not stand alone, but "a man of the Lord." Examples of prophets transmitting the word of the Lord to the nation include the attempts by Moses "the archetypal prophet" (Exodus 3:11–12; 4:10–17) and Jeremiah (Jeremiah 1:4–9) to evade the mission that was given to them and their obligation to fulfill it.

[7]Amos 7:14-15.

[8]2 Kings 18:1-6; 22:2.

[9]Genesis 11:4.

[10]Naftali Zvi Berlin, *Ha'amek Davar* (Jerusalem: Yeshiva of Volozhoin, 1999), 101.

[11]Aristotle, *On the Heavens* (Whitefish: Kessinger Publishing, LLC, 2004), 23.

[12]*Supra* note 10 at 150.

[13]John Stuart Mill, *On Liberty* (Ontario, Canada: Batoche Books, 2001), 18-19.

[14]*Supra* note 10 at 150.

[15]Ibid.

[16]Ibid.

◇◇◇◇◇◇◇◇◇◇◇◇◇◇◇◇◇◇◇◇◇◇◇◇◇◇◇

Bibliography

Aristotle. *On the Heavens.* Whitefish: Kessinger Publishing, LLC, 2004.

Ashkenazi, Shimon. *Yalkut Shim'oni on the Torah.* Jerusalem: Jerusalem Institute, 2006. (In Hebrew)

Berlin, Naftali Zvi. *Ha'amek Davar.* Jerusalem: Yeshiva of Volozhoin, 1999. (In Hebrew)

Chafee, Zechariah. *Freedom of Speech and Press.* New York: Carrie Chapman Catt Memorial Fund, 1955.

Loew, Judah Aryeh. *Be'er Hagolah.* Tel Aviv: Pardes, 1955. (In Hebrew)

Laytner, Anson. *Arguing with God: A Jewish Tradition.* Lanham, MD: Rowman & Littlefield, 1990.

Mill, John Stuart. *On Liberty.* Ontario, Canada: Batoche Books, 2001.

ABOUT THE AUTHORS

Diana I. Bowen is assistant professor of communication studies in the Department of Arts and Humanities at the University of Houston-Downtown in Houston, Texas. She holds a doctor of philosophy degree from The University of Texas at Austin and a master's degree from Syracuse University. Her research interests include archival research, rhetorical theory and criticism, social movements, visual and popular culture, and Latina/o studies. She examined the Gloria Evangelina Anzaldúa Papers located at the Benson Latin American Collection at The University of Texas at Austin and the role of the archive and repertoire in the creation of theories of social change "from below." She teaches rhetoric and public address, communication law and ethics, argumentation and debate, visual rhetoric, and public memory and rhetorical criticism courses. She is currently involved with the Center for Public Deliberation and teaches a course with a summer study abroad program in Paris and Venice.

Daniel S. Brown, Jr. is a professor of communication studies at Pennsylvania's Grove City College where he specializes in media and culture, communication theory, and rhetorical criticism. An Ohio native with an undergraduate degree in religion, he was educated at Miami and Edinboro universities before earning his doctor of philosophy degree from Louisiana State University. Brown took post-doctoral work at The Ohio State University and was a fellow at Northwestern University's Institute on the Holocaust and Jewish Civilization. His essays have appeared in the *Journal of Communication and Religion, Review of Communication, Communication Teacher, Communication Education,* and the *Christian Library Journal.* Brown's research focuses on developing hope analysis, an application of Snyder's hope theory to the communicative arts; interpreting mediated representations of the Holocaust; and exploring interfaith dialogue from interpersonal as well as organization perspectives.

Kenneth R. Chase is chair and associate professor of communication at Wheaton College, in Illinois, where he teaches communication ethics, rhetorical theory, and public speaking. He has served as director of Wheaton's Center for Applied Christian Ethics, president of the Religious Communication Association, and chair of the Communication Ethics Division of the National Communication Association. His scholarly publications explore secular and Christian models of ethical rhetorical practice. He is co-editor (with Alan Jacobs) of *Must Christianity be Violent? Reflections on History, Practice, and Theology.*

Gerald W. C. Driskill is a professor of speech communication at the University of Arkansas at Little Rock where he coordinates the Applied Communication Studies graduate program. Driskill earned his doctor of philosophy degree from the University of Kansas. He teaches communication theory, organizational culture, and intercultural communication. Growing from a campus interfaith dialogue process, he has coordinated workshops designed to enhance the interfaith dialogue skills of students from the FATA region in Pakistan. He relies on the coordinated management of meaning to improve organizational and intercultural communication. His recent research involves the study of community service, church unity, and collaboration.

Kathleen M. Edelmayer is chair and professor of communication at Madonna University in suburban Detroit, where she directs the undergraduate program in interdisciplinary studies and the master's program in liberal studies. Madonna is a Catholic, Franciscan university, founded and operated by the Felician Sisters. Edelmayer's doctorate is from Wayne State University. In 2009 Edelmayer was elected second vice president of the Religious Communication Association. In 2011 she succeeded to the presidency of the RCA. RCA provides opportunities and support to interact and collaborate in ways that truly embody a community of scholars.

Paul Fortunato has published a book about Oscar Wilde's aesthetics, *Modernist Aesthetics and Consumer Culture in the Writings of Oscar Wilde* (Routledge, 2007). He continues to work on Wilde's aesthetics, using phenomenology as a way of articulating how Wilde conceives how works of art function in society. He also works on post-secular theory, including the writing of Jurgen Habermas,

Charles Taylor, and Tariq Ramadan. Fortunato has taught English at the University of Houston-Downtown since 2005. He also is co-director of the University of Houston-Downtown's Center for Public Deliberation, where he promotes discussions on current issues, particularly on interfaith dialogue.

John Gribas is professor and program coordinator of communication and rhetorical studies at Idaho State University. He also serves as the ombudsperson for ISU faculty. His interests relate to language and cognition generally and currently focus on the role of metaphor in the contemporary Christian church. He has worked as a consultant and trainer for various organizations including high-tech production companies, law firms, advertising agencies, military and educational government entities, as well as not-for-profit organizations such as mental health clinics and community theaters. Gribas earned his doctor of philosophy degree from the University of Kansas.

Jeffrey B. Kurtz is associate professor of communication at Denison University in Granville, Ohio, where he teaches courses in the history and criticism of American public address, the rhetoric of social movements, communication theory, research methods in communication, and other areas of special interest. His articles and review essays have been published in the *Review of Communication, the Quarterly Journal of Speech, Rhetoric and Public Affairs, Relevant Rhetoric: A New Journal of Rhetorical Studies, and the Southern Journal of Communication,* among others. Jeff currently is at work on a book manuscript that will examine the intersection of rhetoric, violence, and the American moral imagination. He lives in Granville with his wife, Laura, and their daughters, Eliza and Emerson.

Elizabeth W. McLaughlin is associate professor and chair of communication at Bethel College in Indiana. She holds a doctor of philosophy degree in communication studies from Regent University in Virginia Beach, Virginia, and a master's degree in ministry from Bethel College. Prior to teaching, McLaughlin was a partner of an advertising and public relations firm, served several agencies in copy and account work, as well as four non-profits in public relations management. McLaughlin teaches rhetoric, theory and research, public relations, interpersonal and intercultural communication and writing and public speaking courses. Her essays and articles have appeared in the *Journal of Communication and Religion, Priscilla Papers,* and the *Africanus Journal.* McLaughlin has worked with local women's organizations, a maternity home, and serves on several boards. In addition, she sings in the church choir and enjoys occasional recreational fencing.

Mark R. Orten is a graduate of the University of North Carolina at Chapel Hill with a B.A. in psychology. He earned a master of divinity degree from Princeton Theological Seminary in 1992 and served for eleven years as Presbyterian Campus Minister to Princeton University. Orten came to Denison University in Granville, Ohio, in 2003 to serve as the University Chaplain and director at The Open House: Center for Religious and Spiritual Life, which he founded in 2009.

Rabbi Dr. Tsuriel Rashi is head of the Department of Mass Communications at Lifshitz College of Education in Jerusalem. In the School of Communications at Bar-Ilan University, he serves as graduate academic advisor and as associate director of the Center for Media and Religion. Dr. Rashi is a graduate of Bar-Ilan's Division of Journalism and Communications and holds a master's degree in Political Science/Public Communications as well as a doctor of philosophy degree from that university, the last for his dissertation entitled, "Media, Judaism and Ethics: The Public's 'Duty to Know' in Jewish Law." His principal research interests are related to mass communication and Judaism, education and media, and religious society and the mass media. Rashi developed an instructional program for Jewish religious schools, commissioned by Israel's Ministry of Education, dealing with Judaism and Communications, which is now incorporated into the curricula. He is also chairman of the committee that reshapes the communications, cinema, and theater studies curricula in Israel's religious high schools. Rashi is currently a post-doctoral fellow at Tel-Aviv University, working with Professor Asa Kasher. He has recently published with Professor Maxwell McCombs several articles which addressed agenda setting and religious movements. His fields of interest are Religion and Communication, Jewish Law, Philosophy, and Media Ethics.

Jacob H. Stutzman is an assistant professor of rhetoric and the director of forensics at Oklahoma City University. He completed his doctor of philosophy degree in communication studies from the University of Kansas. Stutzman teaches courses in public address, argumentation and debate, rhetorical criticism, and political communication. Stutzman leads and participates in religious discussion on campus as the founding advisor for the Jewish Student Organization. His research focuses on the mutual influences between religion and politics, and he is currently writing a book on alternative rhetorics of Zionism.

David B. Stern is a lecturer in the Department of Communication Studies at Frostburg State University in Maryland, where he teaches courses on interpersonal communication, language and culture, and public speaking. He is also assisting his department in a grant-funded redesign of the basic human communication course, and serves as faculty advisor to Frostburg's Hillel chapter. Stern is working on his doctoral dissertation on interfaith dialogue at Duquesne University and earned his master's degree from West Chester University of Pennsylvania. He has presented his research on Jewish rhetoric, Jewish communication ethics, and hacker communities as faith communities at the annual conferences of the National Communication Association, Eastern Communication Association, and Pennsylvania Communication Association. Stern also serves on the executive board of the Mountainside Community Mediation Center in Cumberland, Maryland.

Joel S. Ward is currently a visiting instructor at Bethel University and a Ph.D. candidate in the Department of Communication and Rhetorical Studies at Duquesne University. He holds a master's degree in rhetoric and philosophy from Duquesne University and a B.A. in English Literature. Prior to entering doctoral studies Ward worked as a volunteer with Mennonite Central Committee as a Community Livestock Researcher in Noakhali, Bangladesh. His interests include intercultural communication, and he is published in the *Encyclopedia of Identity* on "Third World Identity." Other research interests are crisis communication and the rhetoric of economy. His current dissertation project is on the relationship of the author and hero in the work of Mikhail Bakhtin.

INDEX